FATAL

EXAM

FATAL EXAM

SOLVING LUBBOCK'S GREATEST MURDER MYSTERY

ALAN BURTON & CHUCK LANEHART

TEXAS TECH UNIVERSITY PRESS

This book is typeset in EB Garamond. The paper used in this book meets the minimum requirements of ANSI/NISO Z39.48-1992 (R1997). ♾

Designed by Hannah Gaskamp
Cover design by Hannah Gaskamp

Library of Congress Cataloging-in-Publication Data

Names: Burton, Alan, 1956– author. | Lanehart, Chuck, 1952– author. Title: Fatal Exam: Solving Lubbock's Greatest Murder Mystery / Alan Burton and Chuck Lanehart. Description: Lubbock, Texas: Texas Tech University Press, [2023] | Includes bibliographical references. | Summary: "The true crime account of a notorious murder on the campus of Texas Tech University"—Provided by publisher.
Identifiers: LCCN 2023013335 (print) | LCCN 2023013336 (ebook) |
ISBN 978-1-68283-187-8 (paperback) | ISBN 978-1-68283-188-5 (ebook)
Subjects: LCSH: Murder—Texas—Lubbock. | Texas Tech University.
Classification: LCC HV6534.L83 B878 2023 (print) | LCC HV6534.L83 (ebook) |
DDC 364.152/309764847—dc23/eng/20230829
LC record available at https://lccn.loc.gov/2023013335
LC ebook record available at https://lccn.loc.gov/2023013336

Texas Tech University Press
Box 41037
Lubbock, Texas 79409-1037 USA
800.832.4042
ttup@ttu.edu
www.ttupress.org

To the Keelings and JBC
A. B.

To the memory of my mentor and law partner, the late,
great Byron "Lawyer" Chappell
C. L.

CONTENTS

ILLUSTRATIONS · IX

PROLOGUE · XI

1: December 4, 1967 **/** 3

2: Fear on Campus **/** 19

3: Stakeout, Chase, and Capture **/** 37

4: Who Is Benjamin Lach? **/** 57

5: Wheels of Justice **/** 79

6: Rusk State Hospital **/** 91

7: On Trial **/** 101

8: The Verdict **/** 127

9: The Court of Appeals **/** 133

10: A Model Prisoner **/** 143

11: Parole Bids **/** 163

12: The Education of a Free Man **/** 173

Epilogue **/** 185

CONTENTS

POSTSCRIPT • 201

ACKNOWLEDGMENTS • 213

AUTHORS' NOTES • 215

REFERENCES • 221

ILLUSTRATIONS

5   TTU holiday tradition Carol of Lights
8   Sarah Alice Morgan, custodian at Texas Tech in 1967
9   David Schmidly, graduate teaching assistant in 1967
13   John Hightower and Macie Mathis in the Science Building lab (Room 304-J) where Sarah Alice Morgan was found
15   Sarah Alice Morgan
20   Texas Tech campus map, 1967–1968
21   Science Building as it looked in 1967
22   Construction of the Science Building was completed in 1950–1951
24   Texas Tech students on campus, 1967
25   Front-page headlines, *Lubbock Avalanche-Journal*, December 5, 1967
27   Dr. Grover Murray
28   J. T. Alley, longtime Lubbock police chief
38   Dr. Kent Rylander with other Tech faculty members, 1979
42   *Lubbock Avalanche-Journal* headlines, day after the arrest of Benjamin Lach
43   Lubbock Police Chief J. T. Alley escorting Benjamin Lach to jail
47   Sgt. J. D. Fortner and Chief Bill Daniels, Texas Tech Security Office
58   Benjamin Lach official mugshot
60   Benjamin Lach graduated from Suffolk University
63   Boardinghouse where Benjamin Lach lived in 1967–1968

65   Composite drawing of murder suspect; mug shot of Benjamin Lach

68   C. G. Bartley, Alton Griffin, Edward Sherry, Sal Ingenere

71   Dave Knapp, *Lubbock Avalanche-Journal* police reporter, 1967

73   Benjamin Lach with science students, spring 1968

78   *The Activist Forum*

82   Benjamin Lach and Lubbock Sheriff's Deputy Jim Howard

83   Mrs. Herman Lach outside the courtroom after a hearing

94   Benjamin Lach returning to Lubbock for a sanity hearing, 1970

97   Benjamin Lach escorted out of the 99th District courtroom

103   Lubbock County Criminal District Attorney Blair Cherry

105   Alton Griffin, special prosecutor in the Benjamin Lach trial

115   Texas Tech Police Chief Bill Daniels and secretary Mary Ann Grandjean

129   *University Daily* headline on the conviction of Benjamin Lach

134   Houston attorney Carl Dally

153   Benjamin Lach with friend, Texas Prison Rodeo, Huntsville

154   Benjamin Lach, prison rodeo

155   Benjamin Lach, editor of *The Echo* newspaper while in prison

175   Benjamin Lach released from prison in 1983

187   Science Building today

188   Office 324 shown in the early 2000s; Professor Kent Rylander's office in 1967

189   Current view, north wing hallway, third floor of the Science Building

190   Room 304-J, a lab in 1967; now Room 331, a graduate student office

192   Sign marking the entrance to the City of Lubbock Cemetery

196   Carol of Lights, December 2, 2022

PROLOGUE

ON MONDAY, DECEMBER 4, 1967, A BODY WAS discovered in the Science Building of the largest university in West Texas. The scene was gruesome: the bloody body of the nearly decapitated victim lay lifeless on the cold, hard floor of a laboratory; nearby were a scalpel and broken bone saw, an aquarium, and eyeglasses.

On December 5, 1967, citizens of Lubbock gathered for the Carol of Lights. Typically, this would be the centerpiece of the holidays in this quiet college town, but this year, the usual excitement and anticipation would be shockingly and swiftly shattered by the harrowing events that occurred just twenty-four hours earlier . . .

FATAL EXAM

CHAPTER 1

DECEMBER 4, 1967

WHEN SARAH "ALICE" MORGAN DID NOT SHOW up for dinner, Macie Mathis went searching for her friend and coworker. The two middle-aged women were members of a six-person custodial staff responsible for cleaning the three-story Science Building at Texas Technological College.

Monday, December 4, had dawned cloudy and chilly in Lubbock, Texas, with a chance of rain and a high-temperature forecast to be in the 50s. While sipping coffee and digesting their morning edition of the *Lubbock Avalanche-Journal* (*A-J*), readers were greeted with such front-page headlines as "Heart Transplant Success" and "Red Guerillas in Bold Attack." Those diverse news stories referred to the world's first heart transplant, performed the preceding day by South African surgeon Dr. Christiaan Barnard, and a Saigon battle in the Vietnam War.

That particular morning, Macie Mathis and a seemingly troubled Alice Morgan chatted on the telephone. In a cryptic comment, Morgan told her friend about the recent purchase of a new vacuum cleaner but said she didn't think she would ever get to use it.

The Science Building's entire custodial crew, working the 6 p.m. to 2:30 a.m. shift, typically gathered for an eight o'clock dinner break in the custodians' room on the ground floor of the building. Mathis, working on the second floor, knew her colleague had been assigned the task of cleaning offices and laboratories on the third floor—in most cases, Morgan was the only custodian on the top floor, and she didn't like being alone.

At first, Mathis showed little concern, thinking the fifty-four-year-old might have gone home for supper to check on a sick daughter who was staying with Morgan and her husband. But after noticing Morgan's coat and lunch pail still in the custodians' room and sensing something unusual, she proceeded swiftly to the third floor.

Reaching her destination, Mathis spotted Morgan's trash cart sitting in the hallway outside Room 304-J, a biology laboratory. Still not seeing her coworker, who she thought might have fallen asleep in the lab, Mathis attempted to unlock the door to 304-J, later recalling she "had an awful time with it."

DECEMBER 5, 1967

On the following evening, Texas Tech's ninth annual "Carol of Lights" attracted a large crowd to the quadrangle fronting the Science Building in the center of the massive campus. An annual event since 1959, students and townspeople gather for the celebration, which traditionally marks the beginning of the holiday season on the Lubbock campus and is sponsored by the Residence Hall Association. The Carol of Lights was the brainchild of Harold Hinn, a member of the college's board of directors. That first year, approximately 5,000 lights—all at Hinn's personal expense—decorated the buildings around the circle during Christmas vacation. After that initial event, the lights were displayed before the students left the campus for the holidays.

The Carol of Lights is a holiday tradition at Texas Tech, with its origins dating to 1959. (Courtesy Southwest Collection/Special Collections Library, Texas Tech University [hereafter the Southwest Collection], Photographic Services Collection, U236.1, image 120874.1.)

On this particular unseasonably warm fifty-seven-degree December night, the Tech Choir sang such traditional Christmas carols as "Do You Hear What I Hear?", "O Come All Ye Faithful," "The Little Drummer Boy," and "White Christmas." A dance group, under the direction of Mrs. Suzanne Aker of the physical education department, stood near the arches on each side of the Science Building and presented an interpretation of "Good King Wenceslas." After a fanfare sounded by the Brass Choir, directed by David Payne, the entire campus went dark.

The holiday lights brightened the campus at 7:35 p.m. as the crowd of 10,000 people looked on in celebration. The Tech Choir sang "We Wish You a Merry Christmas," as 17,000 red, yellow, and white lights shined dramatically on thirteen academic buildings, including the Science Building.

With all the activities associated with the Carol of Lights in progress, more than three dozen police officers, including off-duty Lubbock patrolmen and members of the college's security force, kept the ceremony under close scrutiny. According to the *A-J*, officers reported no unusual incidents throughout the evening.

Meanwhile, Bill G. Daniels, the sturdy, soft-spoken forty-six-year-old chief of the college's security police force, said maximum security was in place on campus and "will be maintained for the next few days. People are real jittery, especially the women students. We've taken precautions to protect them a little closer."

To that end, Mrs. Dorothy Garner, coordinator of women's housing, issued a directive to women's residence halls to lock all but one outside door after dark and not to open the wing doors until daylight. This instruction was in addition to the standard rules in place that strictly regulated the times when men could visit women in their dorms.

All these precautions were deemed necessary after the unthinkable and shocking event that had occurred just twenty-four hours earlier on the third floor of the Science Building in the lab—Room 304-J—of Assistant Biology Professor Dr. Francis Rose.

DECEMBER 4, 1967—THE PREVIOUS DAY

That afternoon, at half-past two, Alice Morgan, her husband Richard, and the youngest of their two daughters, twenty-nine-year-old Doris Perry—married and living in Abilene but staying with her parents—enjoyed a hearty lunch at the family's east Lubbock residence. The home-cooked meal consisted of pork chops, corn, spinach, and mashed potatoes.

Some three-and-a-half hours later, the custodial crew gathered for its shift in the Science Building. According to several reports, Morgan arrived about 5:47 p.m. but, for some unknown reason, did not enter the building until 6:05 p.m. Other custodians recalled that she "looked white as a ghost." Normally a very chatty person, "talking a mile a minute," Morgan was said to be in a subdued mood that December evening. Shortly before beginning her shift, she saw Macie Mathis for a brief moment.

With Monday evening classes in session, Dr. Francis Rose exited his lab (Room 304-J) with the door unlocked at approximately 6:30 p.m., on the way to lecture at a seven o'clock biology class on the second floor.

The thirty-two-year-old professor wore dark horn-rimmed glasses, matching the style of the day. He joined the college's faculty the previous year, after having earned his bachelor's and master's degrees at the University of Georgia and his PhD at Tulane University.

Fellow custodian Glenna Morgan saw Alice Morgan at some point on the first floor, and just a few minutes later, at about 6:45 p.m., Tech graduate student Marilyn Ehrlich and her sixteen-month-old daughter arrived on the third floor. They were patiently waiting on Marilyn's husband, Tracy, also a graduate student, to finish research work in his third-floor office.

In the meantime, Marilyn, daughter in tow, stopped to chat with Alice Morgan, who, by now, was standing in the south end of the hallway. The gray-haired Morgan, clad in her light blue uniform dress and light tan shoes, sported thick eyeglasses. She wore a watch, some rings, and, as usual, carried a coin purse in her right dress pocket, which contained four dimes and a penny, a Tech identification card and three other ID cards, a list of bills paid/due, a plastic photograph holder, and a pack of Raleigh filter-tip cigarettes. Pinned to her right dress pocket were her keys.

The two women visited for about five minutes when, at about 6:55 p.m., Tracy Ehrlich emerged from his office to meet his family in the hall, and the Ehrlichs left the building.

According to reports, Morgan was last seen about 7:30 p.m., cleaning Room 308 before proceding to 304-J.

About that time, many Lubbockites joined millions of other Americans relaxing in their homes that winter night, watching the

Sarah Alice Morgan was working as a custodian at Texas Tech in 1967. (Courtesy the Southwest Collection, *University Daily* 46, no. 47.)

popular *I Love Lucy* show on CBS television from 7:30 to 8 p.m. In this particular episode, Lucy was entering an airline stewardess school where her roommate (guest star Carol Burnett) had a fear of heights.

Back in the busy Science Building, roughly between 7:30 p.m. and 7:45 p.m., two graduate teaching assistants—twenty-eight-year-old Frank Judd and twenty-three-year-old David Schmidly—left Rose's second floor lecture.

"I remember that night vividly," Schmidly said years later. (He would one day serve as president of Texas Tech.) "Dr. Rose was teaching a graduate course next door to our office on the second floor. Rose told Frank and me to go upstairs [to Rose's third-floor lab] and mix some chemicals for his zoology lab the next day. We went upstairs and tried to enter the lab to mix the chemicals and it was locked."

David Schmidly was a graduate teaching assistant in 1967 who, along with another TA, unsuccessfully tried to enter Room 304-J while the murder was being committed. (Courtesy the Southwest Collection, Photographic Services Faculty Portraits Collection, U236.1, box 2, envelope 26, image 6-1.)

When they reached the lab at about 7:45 p.m., they noticed a custodian's trash cart in the hall next to the door. After finding the door to Room 304-J locked, the two teaching assistants shook the doorknob and banged on the door. Failing to gain entrance or to elicit a response, they checked the other labs on the floor, which were all apparently locked. Assuming the custodian was on break and because they had not noticed anyone wandering the hallways, the two returned to Rose's lecture on the second floor.

The third floor of the Science Building contained offices and research labs for graduate work; Room 304-J was an aquatic research lab just recently assigned to Rose. Located in the north attic of the building, the twelve-foot-by-fourteen-foot room featured a gabled ceiling, thick walls, and, notably, no windows.

"There is very little traffic in the north end of the attic, where the room is located," observed Dr. Paul Prior, a biology professor, who, like Rose, was lecturing that night on the second floor. "The stairs on that end are used very little and one is just not aware of what is going on up there."

By this time, custodial supervisor John C. Hightower had joined Macie Mathis in the hunt for Alice Morgan. Hurriedly on the way to Room 304-J, they stopped in the lab across the hall to ask Jane Reddell, a part-time lab employee of assistant professor of biology James Wall, if she had seen Morgan. Reddell, who arrived on the third floor shortly after eight o'clock, replied that she had not.

Mathis then proceeded to 304-J and, when she finally managed to unlock the door, discovered the lifeless body of Alice Morgan lying face up on the floor in a pool of blood. Mathis said she "froze" when she saw the body; the time was approximately 8:15 p.m.

"She was lying where I could see her feet as I looked inside the door," Mathis said. "A refrigerator was hiding the rest of her body. . . . All I could see were her legs and the blood. I guess I'll remember that all my life."

After making the gruesome discovery, Mathis frantically summoned her supervisor.

"My God, her throat has been cut," Hightower said, in viewing the body.

He quickly instructed Mathis to call the police, but in her state of anxiety, she instead dialed the campus operator.

There was some confusion when the call for help came in, as the initial Lubbock police report (excerpted below) listed the incident as an "attempted suicide."

I, Officer [Kenneth Ray] Vaughn, received a call by police radio that there was a possible attempted suicide on the third floor of the Science Building at Texas Tech. I received the call at about 8:35 p.m. When I arrived at the scene, the Tech Security Officers James Middlebrook and Willis Jr. were already there and had the area secured and were keeping the people back from the immediate scene and were keeping the people on the third floor from leaving. I went into the room and saw that it was probably murder and that the woman was obviously dead. I called the PD by phone and requested that the Justice of the Peace, the ID Wagon, and other assistance be sent.

When observing the horrible scene in 304-J, police discovered Morgan had nearly been decapitated. "An attempt was made to cut her head off," said a Lubbock police detective. According to later police reports, the body was lying about four feet inside the room from the only door. Morgan's eyeglasses, which she always wore because she "couldn't see anything" without them, lay folded some distance away from the body on the floor, containing diluted blood.

Officers spotted a scalpel and bone saw—both routine lab equipment items—near the body, the saw broken into four pieces. An aquarium, apparently cleaned and emptied, was also in close proximity to the body. The aquarium had contained mud and salamanders, which had been dumped on the floor. Blood splattered the walls and floor of the lab, making the scene indeed graphic. Blood was also visible on the doorknob and in the hallway outside; a cheesecloth used by the custodians was found, with blood stains, near the door.

In the meantime, unaware of anything out of the ordinary, Judd and Schmidly were back on the second floor.

"We went back downstairs and waited until Rose's class was over [about 8:05 p.m.]," Schmidly said. "When he came out of the lecture, we told him that the lab was locked and we couldn't get in."

On hearing that news, Rose was not happy, saying he knew he had left the lab unlocked and/or the door open.

"We [Schmidly, Judd, and Rose] went back up there [to 304-J]," Schmidly said.

But en route, an anxious Jane Reddell stopped Rose in the third-floor hallway.

"I'm so glad you're here," she told the professor.

"I'm just going to my lab."

"I don't really think you want to go in there!"

"Why not?"

"Because there's blood all over the place."

"What in the hell are you talking about?"

"The cleaning woman has killed herself."

Rose continued on to his lab, where he met custodial supervisor John Hightower and asked, "What happened?"

"She cut her throat."

"Can we do anything to help her?"

"Nothing can be done for her."

Rose then looked at the murder scene and stepped back into the hall.

"She wouldn't do this to herself. This looks like murder. Has anyone called the police?"

"Macie is."

Schmidly later recalled that "there was blood on the door. . . . We then saw Mrs. Morgan laying on the floor and the blood, water, and salamanders. It was a gruesome sight. Frank [Judd] and I later realized that [the murderer] was probably in the lab doing that [the killing] when we were knocking on the door trying to get in."

An autopsy revealed the wounds to Morgan's neck were clean-cut, as if made by a scalpel, but irregular in their direction, with some superficial adjacent cuts. The skin, soft tissue, muscle, trachea, esophagus,

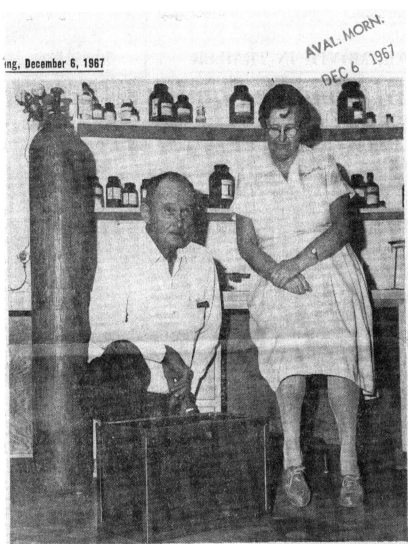

ing, December 6, 1967

AVAL. MORN.
DEC 6 1967

SCENE OF SLAYING—Two Texas Tech employes who found the nearly decapitated body of Mrs. Richard O. Morgan Monday night are shown in the Tech science building laboratory where the grim find was made. They are John Hightower, custodial foreman, and Mrs. Macie Mathis, custodian and co-worker of the victim. In the foreground is an aquarium that played a bizarre and as yet undetermined role in the slaying. (Staff Photo)

Texas Tech custodial foreman John Hightower and custodian Macie Mathis found the body of coworker Sarah Alice Morgan in this lab (304-J) in the Science Building. (*Lubbock Avalanche-Journal* morgue file collection, the Southwest Collection.)

and major vein and artery in the neck were all severed. The report also noted that Morgan sustained a blow to the head, with perhaps a blunt instrument, that caused bruises to the back right side of the head and to the left forehead. The right side of her neck bone was cut about a half inch deep with a coarse rough edge. Small lacerations were visible on the second and third fingers of the left hand. A small bruise was located on the right side of the chest, and bruises were found on the back of both elbows. She was not sexually assaulted.

The only noteworthy item missing from Morgan's person was a set of building keys, issued to all custodial staff; her fellow workers said they were strictly forbidden to unlock any doors for students.

"Mrs. Morgan's key ring had been ripped from her dress," said Ray Downing, director of building maintenance. "It looked as if whoever did it was intent on getting those keys."

Alice Morgan and her husband of thirty-seven years, Richard "Ocie" Morgan, a retired mechanic and fellow Tech custodian, lived a few miles east of the campus in downtown Lubbock near Mackenzie Park. Richard Morgan, working in a nearby campus building at the time of the slaying, said later he was baffled by the theft of the keys.

"[The keys] all belonged to Tech," he said. "There were no personal keys on the reel and none of her personal belongings were missing either. She was in the habit of locking the door behind her while she cleaned the rooms."

It was believed that Alice Morgan possessed four keys and a towel dispenser key. The four keys would have included a general master key (Key No. 80), a key to an outside building she cleaned, a key to several doors in the south attic of the Science Building, and another unknown key.

Strangely enough, on the day *after* the murder, investigators discovered Morgan's Tech ID card and coin purse under a counter in 304-J. Either police overlooked those items on the night of the murder, or they were placed there later by person(s) unknown.

There were conflicting reports as to the normal times Morgan cleaned the third floor rooms: one report indicated that Morgan usually worked

Sarah Alice Morgan. (Author collection.)

on the third floor at about 9 p.m., but another said that she often began work at that location at about 7 p.m.

News about the savage murder spread quickly across campus.

"I was waiting to go for supper when the telephone rang at the *University Daily* (*UD*) [student newspaper] saying there had been a murder in the Science Building," recalled retired newspaper publisher Roy McQueen, who was a *UD* co-managing editor at the time of the murder. "I thought it was a crank call but looked out the window. I could not see the emergency vehicles, but I could see the reflections of the red lights. My wife was waiting for me in the rear of the Journalism Building. I sent her on home and went to the Science Building. A fairly large crowd had already gathered and I was able to peek into the room where there was a massive amount of blood. I could not see how the assailant could have got away without being spattered in blood. I stayed on the police side of the story and my co-managing editor [Jim Davis] went to the funeral home to get information on the victim."

Also recalling the night's shocking events was Dr. Bill Dean, then-director of student publications at Tech and later executive vice president and CEO of the Texas Tech Alumni Association.

"That evening, I went back to the office to do some work," Dean stated. "I noticed police cars in the Science Quadrangle but didn't think too much about it until I attempted to enter the old Journalism Building, where my office was located. The door was locked, which was very unusual for that time of night since *University Daily* reporters were coming and going until the late hours of the evening. I opened the door and was greeted by the custodian who worked in that building. She had locked the door and was carrying a large knife to protect herself. She told me what had happened in a panic-stricken tone. Of course, *UD* staffers were everywhere. It was a wild scene. Each one had a 'theory' about what had happened. . . . I will never forget that evening."

Macie Mathis said later that Morgan had appeared "troubled and worried" in recent days but had attributed that to possible complications surrounding the impending birth of Morgan's grandchild. By most accounts, Morgan liked her job and her fellow workers.

"She was a real talkative person and very cheerful," Mathis said. "She laughed a lot. She always said if she couldn't laugh, she wouldn't want to live."

Meanwhile, Doris Perry, the Morgans' expectant daughter, sat alone in their Lubbock home Monday night watching television. That was how she learned of the murder: although the local TV news report did not release the name of the victim, the daughter knew instantly it was her mother.

Beverly Barnes, daughter of Doris Perry and granddaughter of Alice Morgan, recalled years later in an interview that her "grandmother had told her [Doris Perry] before leaving for work that night that if she needed her, she'd be on the third floor of the Science Building."

In the days after the murder, Richard Morgan would blame himself for what happened because he had encouraged his wife to take the job at Tech.

SARAH TERA ALICE KNIGHT WAS BORN ON MAY 6, 1913, IN MENA, ARKANSAS. IN 1938, SARAH TERA ALICE KNIGHT MORGAN MOVED TO LUBBOCK, TEXAS, WITH HER HUSBAND, RICHARD MORGAN. THE MORGANS RESIDED AT 2902 EAST FOURTH STREET. MRS. MORGAN TOOK A CUSTODIAL JOB AT TECH IN SEPTEMBER 1966, AND HAD WORKED IN THE SCIENCE BUILDING FOR THE PAST FOUR MONTHS. PRIOR TO THAT, SHE WAS EMPLOYED AT SUNBEAM LAUNDRY, A LOCAL BUSINESS ESTABLISHMENT, FOR APPROXIMATELY THREE YEARS.

SIDEBAR: EXTRA SECURITY ALSO IN FORCE AT 1966 CAROL OF LIGHTS

For an event designed to celebrate the holidays, the Carol of Lights drew more than its share of unsavory attention. The extra security at the festivities in the wake of the Sarah Alice Morgan murder in 1967 proved to be merely a repeat from the previous year.

The 1966 edition of the Carol of Lights was held on Tuesday, December 6. After widespread rumors of "disaster" or "serious trouble," thirty-one policemen were stationed on campus rooftops and in the Science Quadrangle that evening.

Texas Tech officials later confirmed that two men had been detained and another placed under constant surveillance during the ceremony. One of the men had a gun, scope, and ammunition, while another had made a suspicious tape recording.

At least two coeds received threatening phone calls warning them not to attend the Carol of Lights because of impending danger.

"We took every precaution except calling this thing off," Tech President Grover Murray said afterwards. He added that rumors of "somebody just doing something" had been circulating around campus since Thanksgiving and that there had been "a suggestion of serious trouble tonight."

Fortunately, no incidents occurred, and the men were released from custody.

CHAPTER 2

FEAR ON CAMPUS

LUBBOCK, TEXAS, IS NORMALLY A TRANQUIL place, offering an easygoing lifestyle for its friendly, downhome, churchgoing, law-abiding West Texas citizens. For a city with a population of 164,000 in 1967, Lubbock retained that sought-after small-town feel.

Known for its thriving cotton fields, prairie dogs, prolific sandstorms, conservative values, abundant churches, and as the home of rock 'n roll music pioneer Buddy Holly and many other influential musicians, the city of Lubbock is located on the South Plains of West Texas, almost an equal distance—300-plus miles—from Albuquerque, New Mexico, and Dallas, Texas.

The origin of Texas Technological College is a unique story as well.

Early in the twentieth century, as the western part of Texas rapidly developed, legislators began to consider the establishment of a new college in the region. Thirty-seven communities competed for the coveted prize, including Abilene and Lubbock.

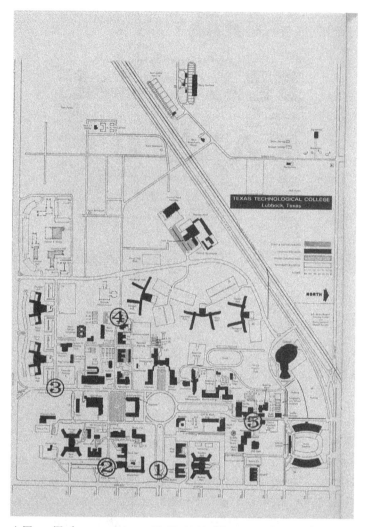

A Texas Tech campus map, 1967–1968. (Courtesy the Southwest Collection, Tips for Tech Men, 1967–1968.)

William Harrison Bledsoe, born in Cleburne, Texas, in 1869, was a pioneer Lubbock lawyer. In 1923, the Lubbock senator authored the bill that established Texas Technological College in Lubbock, to "give instruction in technological, manufacturing, and agricultural pursuits" and "to elevate the ideals, enrich the lives, and increase the capacity of the people for democratic self-government."

The Science Building as it looked in 1967. Original plans for the location of the Science Building called for the construction of the Hall of Texas, a state-of-the-art facility that would house an auditorium and commencement hall. Those lofty plans were later scrapped, and the Science Building was built in its place in 1951. (Courtesy 1967 *La Ventana* yearbook, author collection.)

The Lubbock Steering Committee purchased 2,008 acres of land just west of the city and sold it to the state. Texas Technological College opened on September 30, 1925, with 914 students and six buildings. Initially it had four schools: Agriculture, Engineering, Home Economics, and Liberal Arts.

By 1967, Texas Tech's enrollment topped 18,000 students in seven schools, including Law.

Entering the 399-acre campus from Broadway Street and heading west just past Memorial Circle, a visitor to the college in 1967 would have headed into a cul-de-sac known as the "Science Quadrangle," which included the Social Science Building, Science Building, and Chemistry Building. Heading back east around the circle and to the south stands the Administration Building.

The Science Building, with its light-brown brick and red tile roof, fits in easily with the Spanish Renaissance architecture prevalent throughout

Construction of the Science Building was completed in 1950–1951. (Author collection.)

campus. The ornate structure, reminiscent of an old high school or public library, features decorative archways on either side of an impressive, elevated stair entrance and seven exterior doors. Completed in 1951, the Science Building was not one of the campus's thirteen original main buildings. The initial plans for the location of the Science Building called for the construction of the "Hall of Texas" or "Alamo Memorial Hall," a state-of-the-art facility that would house an auditorium and commencement hall. Those lofty plans were later scrapped, and the Science Building appeared in its place.

A more architecturally technical description of the building is offered by Brian Griggs in *Opus in Brick and Stone: The Architectural and Planning History of Texas Tech University* (2020):

[Architect] Emmett Koeppe's design for the Science Building featured a blend of hip-and-gable clay tile clad roof forms set atop yet another three-story C-shaped plan, albeit with two asymmetrical west wings. At the center of the building a single four-story form broke the clay tile roofs whose general form may have been inspired by [Wyatt] Hedrick's recently completed Veterans Affairs Hospital in Amarillo.

Not everyone was impressed by the design of what was originally envisioned to be the great Hall of Texas. In *The First Thirty Years* (1956), Ruth Horn Andrews wrote: "At the end of the campus drive leading out of Lubbock's splendid wide street, appropriately called Broadway, there stands not the envisioned Hall of Texas, but a squatty structure of anomalous design denominated the Science Building." Griggs countered that opinion in his book, writing: "Regardless of Ruth Horn Andrews' sharp criticism . . . today, particularly among the public, the Science Building has become a cherished part of Tech heritage, namely due to the centerpiece role it plays in the annual Carol of Lights Festival."

From a historical perspective, 1967 might be best described as a year of turmoil across the United States. As the Vietnam War raged, anti-war demonstrations were in full force back home, with protestors voicing their growing discontent loud and clear about not only the war but also President Lyndon B. Johnson. Quite frequently, college campuses turned out to be popular sites for such public displays—"Peace" was in, the "Establishment" was out.

The times they were a-changin', but the times were also turbulent. There's no question that America was a country undergoing dramatic change in 1967—from politics to civil rights to music to fashion to drugs and beyond. The year was anything but dull deep in the heart of Texas, as weather, business, politics, and sports competed for attention.

Despite the discontent and turmoil at many college campuses around the country, Texas Tech enjoyed a relatively calm existence in the late

Texas Tech students enjoy a relaxing moment on campus
in 1967. (Courtesy *La Ventana* yearbook.)

1960s—with rare exceptions. In May 1967, campus protestors rallied to
change the name of Texas Technological College to either Texas State
University or Texas Tech University. (The Texas Legislature finally and
officially changed the name to Texas Tech University two years later.)

But as protests go, it was no Cal–Berkeley.

In fact, it is not hard to imagine Norman Rockwell feeling right at
home on the Lubbock campus during that era. Perhaps he'd sketch
a handsome young football player in his Double T letter jacket and
Wranglers, standing on the steps of Stangel Hall (a new air-conditioned
dorm) courting a pretty coed, the subjects oblivious as a sandstorm
swirls in the background.

But in the wake of the murder of Tech custodian Alice Morgan, the
patrons at Bob's Café on Main Street across from campus were no doubt

LUBBOCK AVALANCHE-JOURNAL

"FIRST In Lubbock—FIRST On The South Plains"

46th Year No. 30   30 Pages   Lubbock, Texas, Tuesday Morning, Dec. 5, 1967   Full Leased Wires: (AP), (UPI)

CLEANING EMPLOYE'S THROAT CUT

Woman Murdered At Tech

LBJ Names New Marine Skipper

Killer May Be Thrill Slayer

Mrs. Alice Morgan, 54, Is Victim In Laboratory Of Science Building

BUT CRUCIAL PERIOD LOOMS

'I'm Feeling Much Better,' Says Man With New Heart

'Kid' Tales Of Cabinet Change Hit

President Makes New Pitch For Tax Bill

VIETNAM WAR

Bomb Buying Hints At New Escalation

MERGER WEAPONS

Front-page headlines of the *Lubbock Avalanche-Journal* on December 5, 1967, the day after the murder of Alice Morgan. (*Lubbock Avalanche-Journal* morgue file collection, the Southwest Collection.)

abuzz with talk Tuesday morning about the previous night's events that suddenly left the city and Tech gripped in fear.

Gun sales quickly escalated throughout the community, and worried parents from across Texas called to check on their students. In some cases, Tech coeds fearfully returned home to the safety of those parents.

School officials told the *University Daily* that night classes would continue as scheduled, but with Tech police providing maximum security on campus. The twenty-four uniformed Tech officers were well qualified, trained, and commissioned by the Lubbock Police Department. That being said, the campus police, whose department originated in 1959, spent most of their time on routine parking and traffic enforcement, having handed out more than 23,000 tickets the previous year. During that time, new permanent steel-and-glass entry stations were installed at the five entrances to campus, with the purpose of reducing congestion and increasing pedestrian safety.

Violent crime being a rarity, the school nevertheless did its best to offer protection, stationing armed guards around the Science Building each night and utilizing eleven officers to guard the women's dormitories from 10:30 p.m. until 6 a.m. Trusted male students volunteered to escort females to their automobiles at night.

In the early stages of the investigation, however, city and campus police had few, if any, clues.

"Woman Murdered at Tech—Killer May Be Thrill Slayer"—screamed the headlines of the December 5, 1967, *Lubbock Avalanche-Journal*. The lead of the story read as follows: "The body of a woman employee of Texas Tech, her head almost severed, was found in a blood-spattered laboratory on the third floor of the Tech Science building here Monday night. Local police, with practically no clues to the identity of the killer, began their search for what one official labeled a 'thrill slayer.'"

December 6, 1967
University Daily Editorial
"Powerful Force of Fear"
Fear is a powerful force, and when it grips a community or campus it is both overbearing and demoralizing. And it continues until the source is eliminated. Whether or not this occurred Tuesday night remains to be seen.

That is the situation on the Tech campus now. The atmosphere is one of fear. Women will not walk across campus; men are apprehensive about it. Countless calls come from parents. People lie awake at night thinking about a murder they find difficult to believe. Doors are locked and people are jumpy. The normal life and purpose of the university has been disrupted.

It is ironic, yet very real, that the actions of one person can have such a powerful effect on more than 20,000 persons. Impending danger for each person is actually very minute, but people tend to rule out percentages when personal well-being is involved. To each the danger is imminent.

It will continue to be so until the assailant is apprehended. Only

Dr. Grover Murray enjoyed a distinguished ten-year (1966–1976) career as Texas Tech president. (*Lubbock Avalanche-Journal* morgue file collection, the Southwest Collection.)

then will the grip be released. The "imminent danger" will be gone, but the scar will be here a long time.

"The event set off a panic on this campus," recalled Dr. Bill Dean. "Who had committed this brutal crime, and why? The campus was not nearly as well lighted then as it is now. . . . People were very much on edge. It was a very tense situation."

J. T. Alley was a longtime Lubbock police chief, serving in
that capacity from 1957 to 1983. (*Lubbock Avalanche-Journal*
morgue file collection, the Southwest Collection.)

Jackie Smith, a first-year agricultural economics major at the time
from tiny Roscoe, Texas (located near Abilene in West Texas and with
a population of 1,500 in 1967), remembers taking an exam in the
Engineering Building on the night of the slaying.

"I heard about it from other students that night—I didn't know the gruesome details until the next day," Smith said years later. "I lived in Gordon
Hall, a few hundred yards east of the crime scene. There was panic—some
kids went home and stayed for a few days. Our dorm was never locked, but
after that, they locked it for a few nights. . . . For a farm boy from Roscoe, it
was a pretty big event." Smith was also familiar with the Science Building
as he was taking a biology class and lab in that location.

David Schmidly, one of the two graduate teaching assistants who, unknowingly, nearly interrupted the crime as it was being committed, also recalled the fear in a personal way.

"I was a newlywed at the time, and my wife was scared to death for me to go to work at night up in that [Science] Building," he said. "But that was my job, to work in the building at all hours, so I really had no choice. . . . I didn't take a gun because it was illegal, but I took a hammer with me and put it in my coat [for protection]."

With the murder investigation and public interest ramping up, officials offered two media briefings per day, beginning on Wednesday, December 6. Lubbock District Attorney Alton Griffin, Texas Tech President Grover Murray, Lubbock Captain of Detectives Bill Cox, and Tech Security Chief Bill Daniels all provided updates as information became available.

In doing so, authorities released composite drawings of two men who were wanted for questioning. One of the individuals, reportedly seen in the Science Building at least four times between 6:30 p.m. and 9:30 p.m. on the night of the murder, was described as about twenty-four years old, five foot ten inches tall, 180 pounds, with an olive complexion and dark crew cut. The other man, described as about twenty-one years old, six feet tall, and 165 pounds, had dark hair and wore dark horn-rimmed glasses with light-green lenses.

Lubbock Police Chief J. T. Alley, attired in his usual western garb, which included cowboy boots and string tie, said that fifty to seventy-five persons in or around the Science Building at the time of the slaying had been interviewed. The victim's bloody clothing, fingernail scrapings, hair found on her hands, and other evidence gathered at the crime scene was forwarded for analysis to the FBI laboratory in Washington, DC. Also sent to the FBI was a bloodstained white dress shirt (size 15 1/2-34) discovered in a dumpster on the campus two days after the murder.

Police ruled out robbery and theft as motives, due to money found in Morgan's purse, her jewelry still on her body, and nothing appearing to be missing from the lab. But there was that one troubling exception:

the victim's keys were nowhere to be found. Assuming Morgan had been knocked unconscious at the beginning of the attack, police speculated there may have been no screams for help. Or even if there were, police reasoned, the lab's thick concrete walls would surely have muffled the noise—at least one investigator believed "she was flat on her back when her throat was cut."

Late on Tuesday, December 5, Captain Cox told the *A-J*: "We are desiring any information that could help us in any way—regardless of how trivial it might seem. It might be part of the puzzle we're trying to put together."

Funeral services for Alice Morgan were held at 3 p.m. on Thursday, December 7, 1967, at the Henderson Funeral Directors Chapel in Lubbock. Survivors included her husband, two daughters (Eva Goad of Lubbock and Doris Perry of Abilene), and seven grandchildren. Rev. Bill Widmer and Rev. Royce Womack of the First Methodist Church in Lubbock conducted the services.

"Nothing can remove the loss caused by this tragedy that struck not only a family but also our community," Reverend Womack told the 120 mourners. "But let us remember, it is the quality of life that is important, not the length of it."

Morgan was laid to rest in the City of Lubbock Cemetery.

As the investigation intensified, authorities asked Dr. Francis Rose and Biology Department Chair Dr. Earl Camp to attend the services, hoping one of the men might recognize someone matching the previously released composite drawings. The professors walked up and down the street outside the funeral home, peered into cars, went inside the funeral parlor, and sat in Camp's vehicle as part of their observation process. However, they did not recognize anyone they thought resembled the sketches.

Police also requested two waitresses from the Toddle House restaurant, located at Sixth and College Avenue, to go to the funeral and look for a man who had entered their establishment at 11:30 p.m. on the night of the murder. The unnamed individual was bleeding while in the restaurant. However, the two women did not identify anyone there.

Finally, KLBK-TV news director Duncan Ellison aided investigators. While hidden from view, Ellison took photographs of various persons leaving the funeral chapel on the chance a photo might match one of the composite drawings—to no avail.

Desperate for leads, police went so far as to have Sgt. J. D. Fortner, a Tech police officer, pose as a custodian in the Science Building for a week after the murder. That, too, proved fruitless.

Later in the week, Dr. Murray Kovnar, a clinical psychologist and professor at Texas Tech, offered his analysis of the killer to the police and media.

"The act itself is psychotic," Kovnar said. "It would probably be more homicidal suicide rather than just a psychopath, or it also could be a normal person placed in a stress situation who just lost control of his reasoning power. . . . The crime doesn't necessarily have to have been committed by a person who was psychotic. A psychopath is a person who doesn't have any guilt feelings and who doesn't want to live within the rules of his society. But the crime does indicate a need for psychiatric attention."

Kovnar added this chilling observation: "It certainly would have to be a sick person. There was lots of hostility and lots of aggression there. If properly provoked, I think it is most likely that he is capable of killing again. The hardest thing is to do it the first time. The second time it's easier. . . . There's bound to be a duplication or repetition somewhere . . . but as long as this person is on the loose, he's like a wounded animal and a lot more dangerous. Every homicidal suicide leaves a cry for love or help."

Kovnar even compared the act to two high-profile crimes from the previous year: the murder of sixteen people by University of Texas tower sniper Charles Whitman, and the stabbing/strangulation of eight student nurses in Chicago by Richard Speck.

"[All three crimes] were unjustifiable, but still deliberate," Kovnar said.

Lacking the sophisticated investigative and DNA techniques that would not be available until years later, Lubbock police nevertheless checked out numerous leads in the days after the murder, with the following turning into dead ends:

- On Friday, December 8, a thirty-five-year-old Latin American man flagged down Lubbock patrolmen, telling them: "I'm the man you're looking for. I want to see a psychiatrist." After further investigation, it was determined that the man was not involved in the Morgan murder and in fact was a former mental patient.
- On Sunday, December 10, just six days after the murder of Alice Morgan, another Texas college experienced the shockwaves of a brutal killing. This time it occurred at Baylor University in Waco, Texas, with the discovery of a nineteen-year-old Baylor coed who had been maniacally murdered. The body of Jill Brown, whose throat was slashed (jugular vein severed) and who had been stabbed in the chest (puncturing her heart and lungs), was found in a cedar brush thicket near a marina on Lake Waco. The Crawford, Texas, freshman had been missing for two days. Lubbock and Waco police compared notes but did not see any similarities in the Morgan and Brown cases. A week later, on December 18, a twenty-five-year-old bakery shop employee/Air Force veteran, after giving a statement to authorities, was charged with the Brown murder. Police believed a hunting knife to be the murder weapon. The suspect, Jackie W. Grider, married with a small child, was not linked to the Morgan case.
- On Wednesday, December 13, Lubbock police searched a men's dormitory room at Tech, looking for Morgan's missing keys. After not finding any keys, authorities released the student being questioned.
- On Friday, December 15, the Tech Traffic-Security Office received through the mail an audiotape recording of a person apparently confessing to the Morgan murder. Although Chief Bill Daniels labeled the tape a hoax, he did forward it to Lubbock police. Police Capt. Bill Cox viewed the tape as a "smoke screen" thrown up by an individual who was "showing off more than anything else." He added, "We think we know who made it."

• On Wednesday, December 20, a student who resembled the description of a man observed in the area of the Science Building on the night of the murder passed a polygraph examination.

Richard Morgan, the slain woman's husband, told the *A-J* that the murderer was "hopped up on something and a real nut to start with. He must have been a real maniac. I have no suspects. . . . It could have been, but I don't believe it was anybody she knew. I feel like they'll never catch him with all they've got to go on . . . they may in years to come."

Bobby Davis, a nephew of the Morgans, said: "[The killer] wasn't waiting for Mrs. Morgan. Any woman would have done. There was something in there [the lab] they wanted. They would have killed any woman that came in there."

While both Alice and Richard Morgan were Tech custodians, one of their sons-in-law, Robert Perry, was also previously employed on the school's custodial staff. He had recently moved to Abilene, Texas, approximately 165 miles southeast of Lubbock.

Captain Cox said the probe continued on an "around the clock basis, but we have nothing new. We're still questioning some people, but just haven't come up with anything good yet."

With the 1968 spring semester at Tech set to begin February 5, tight campus security remained in place. "Time is going to hamper the investigation," Cox admitted. "We've been fighting time all along, and it hasn't been in our favor."

A month later, officials decided to take a more aggressive approach, as related in the following article dated February 1 by *A-J* reporter Dave Knapp, who would later play a key role in solving the case:

> Texas Tech and police officials took double-barreled action Wednesday to revitalize the nine-week probe into the bizarre scalpel murder of Mrs. Sarah Alice Morgan, a campus building custodian.
>
> Dr. Grover E. Murray, Tech president, and Police Chief J. T. Alley, noting that there had been no significant developments

in the case, disclosed these moves to intensify and enhance the investigation:

- A $5,000 reward, none of which involves state funds, has been posted for information leading to the arrest and conviction of the person or persons responsible for the murder of the 54-year-old Lubbock woman.
- The aid of the Texas Rangers will be requested by Alley today to set up a concerted effort to break the baffling slaying case. Alley said the Rangers had been kept fully informed on progress to date, but added that they would be furnished with a complete case history as soon as possible.

Murray, admitting that the campus still is a "bit jittery," said he felt the actions would have a psychological effect and will boost morale on the campus. "There's a possibility that someone is holding back some information, just waiting for a reward."

Alley said the police probe had "turned up no one we could classify as a suspect. I hope these moves produce something."

The reward is being offered by five Lubbock banks and was announced by Roy Furr, chairman of the Texas Tech Board of Regents. Pledging the $5,000 were First National Bank, Citizens National Bank, Security National Bank, Lubbock National Bank, and Plains National Bank.

SIDEBAR: THE SHALLOWATER MURDERS

Seven months prior to the murder of Alice Morgan, another grisly crime scene surfaced in small-town Shallowater, Texas, located just a few miles northwest of Lubbock.

In the early morning hours of April 18, 1967, the bodies of D. J. Brown, age fifty-two, and his wife Birdie McCauley Brown, fifty-one, were discovered in their rural farmhouse by sheriff's deputies. Both had been brutally beaten to death with a blunt instrument. The motive appeared to be robbery, as both cash and credit cards were missing from

D. J. "Buzz" Brown, who, in addition to his farming interests, owned an insurance agency.

Later that day, the couple's twenty-five-year-old son was arrested and charged with murder with malice aforethought. The authorities contended that Dolphus Jack Brown, an only child, needed money to pay off debts.

After a change of venue to El Paso County, the son was convicted on October 16, 1968, and sentenced to thirteen years in prison. After his conviction, however, Jack Brown remained free on a $25,000 appeal bond for three years and at one point lived in Dallas before his appeal was denied.

At the trial, a Lubbock physician described Brown as "one of the kindest and gentlest persons I've ever been around."

At the time of the Morgan murder, Brown, a Tech student, was out on bond and living near the campus on Boston Avenue. On the night of the murder, he was identified as having a scratch on his face by two waitresses in a Toddle House coffee shop at Sixth Street and College Avenue, in close proximity to campus. However, police quickly cleared Brown of any involvement in the crime.

Brown finally began serving his prison term in March 1972 and was paroled five years later.

CHAPTER 3

STAKEOUT, CHASE, AND CAPTURE

TIME MOVES ON. BITTER WINTER COLD TURNS TO SPRING sunshine, and at Texas Tech the 1968 spring semester was in full swing.

The good news: there were no additional murders on campus since Alice Morgan was slain on December 4, 1967. The bad news: there was still a killer on the loose somewhere, and the campus and Lubbock community continued to feel a sense of anxiety and uneasiness, while doing their best to resume normal lives.

Investigators continued to work quietly behind the scenes in an effort to solve the baffling mystery.

MARCH 12–13, 1968

A police stakeout, or the hidden surveillance of a location or person(s) in anticipation of a crime, is a tactic utilized since the early 1940s. No

Dr. Kent Rylander, fourth from left, along with other Tech faculty members recognized for their teaching excellence, 1979. (Courtesy the Southwest Collection, Outstanding teachers recognized, 1979–1980, Heritage Club Photograph Collection, image E2004.)

doubt the movies and television have added to the "drama" involved in waiting, watching, and hopefully catching a criminal in the act.

Shortly after dusk on Tuesday, March 12, 1968, Lubbock police detectives Frank Wiley and F. C. "Butch" Hargrave took their stakeout positions in Room 324 of the Texas Tech Science Building. Room 324, the office of Tech Assistant Biology Professor Dr. Michael Kent Rylander, was just down the hall from Room 304-J—the lab where Tech custodian Alice Morgan was brutally murdered on December 4, 1967.

The thirty-two-year-old bespectacled Rylander, recognized as a well-mannered scholar with a gentle nature, grew up on a farm near Denton in North Texas, where his father taught agriculture. Rylander earned his bachelor's and master's degrees at hometown North Texas State University and his PhD at Tulane University, and he joined the Tech faculty in 1965. His major interests included the study of birds and the evolution of the behavior of animals and humans.

The police hastily arranged a stakeout after Rylander alerted Tech security that someone entered his office earlier in the day (March 12) and that a filing cabinet containing an Embryology 332 quiz had been disturbed. Rylander previously announced to his embryology class that he would administer an exam early during the week of March 11–15. The professor kept his exams in a file cabinet and the key to the cabinet in his desk drawer. In his official report to the Tech security office, Rylander wrote:

At 5:00 p.m., March 11 I placed a small piece of paper in the lock of the filing cabinet where my secretary placed a test to be given March 12, the next day. I placed the paper in the lock because I suspected that the lock might be broken into on the night of March 11, and if the paper were missing, I would know that someone had opened the filing cabinet. The next morning, March 12, at 7:30 I checked the filing cabinet to see if it had been opened, and at that time it had not. I went to give my lectures, and noticed, half way through my first lecture, that one of my students, one whom I suspected might be inclined to enter the filing cabinet, came in late. I thought during the lecture that he might have broken into the cabinet during the first part of my lecture, so I checked when I got back from the lecture, and the piece of paper was in fact out of the lock, indicating that the cabinet had been opened. I phoned traffic security who sent an officer to my lab. He carefully took the test and its folder out of the cabinet and took it to Traffic Security office for fingerprinting.

After receiving this information, Tech security notified Lubbock police of the new development and possible connection to the Morgan case. Cooperating with the police and district attorney's office, Rylander then arranged for a second "super tough" examination to be given to his embryology class on Wednesday, March 13, at 5:30 p.m.

Years later, Rylander admitted he got the idea for the filing cabinet "trap" from watching a James Bond movie. His wife told a reporter, "Kent saw the paper-in-the-lock trap on a television detective show."

It was a long shot, but based on this tip, District Attorney Alton Griffin and Lubbock Police Chief J. T. Alley quickly and quietly implemented the stakeout—setting a trap and hoping the individual would return to Rylander's office after hours.

Detectives Wiley and Hargrave waited and waited in Room 324 throughout the night and into the early morning hours of March 12–13. Meanwhile, Rylander, unaware of the plan, had been home, babysitting his two young children, but inadvertently stumbled into the trap.

"That night [of the stakeout], I had to come in [my office] for something," Rylander said in a 2004 interview. "And as I came in, I opened the door and then the two policemen grabbed their guns and started aiming at me—like cowboy fashion. So, I told them it was alright. And so they were, 'no problem.' So, I got what I needed."

At 7:25 a.m. on Wednesday, March 13, the detectives' patience was rewarded. At that time, according to later trial testimony, the two detectives heard footsteps in the hallway.

"A key was put in the lock and the door opened a couple of inches; then it hesitated," Hargrave testified during court proceedings. "After a few seconds, the door opened and he walked in."

"Good morning, Mr. Lach," Detective Wiley greeted the surprised intruder.

With that said, Benjamin Lach "dropped his books and ran out and down the stairs," Hargrave said. Forty years later, Hargrave denied the accusation of some that he and his partner had fallen asleep on the job. "We heard the door rattle and knew he was coming in," Hargrave said. "Back then, Frank [Wiley] and I both smoked [cigarettes] heavily. When [Lach] opened the door, I think he smelled the smoke [and took off]. I didn't see anything but his hand through the slight crack of the door. . . . I was right on his heels, but after he cleared the stairs, I never saw him again. He was a young guy and in very good shape."

The ensuing chase and eventual capture of Benjamin Lach in west Lubbock came straight out of a Keystone Kops episode. In his haste to escape, Lach left a master key in the door of Room 324; also left behind were two library books and a spiral notebook.

Incredibly, he eluded the detectives, bounding down the stairs and out of the Science Building. Leaving behind his bicycle at the building, Lach presumably proceeded on foot some thirty-eight blocks to 47th Street, where he stole an automobile belonging to Judy Beavers. Lach took the car, which was left with the engine running in the driveway of the Beavers' residence, stopped at a service station for gas, and drove off without paying.

From there, the official Lubbock Police Department offense report provides the dramatic details:

A call was put out at 0856 on this date that a 1965 red and white Pontiac with New Mexico license plates had been stolen from 3601 47th St. The stolen car was reported last seen going west on 50th St. and Knoxville Ave. Officer [Emmett] Caddell first observed the car with the above-named subject [Benjamin Lach] as the driver pulling out of the Texaco Station at 50th St. and Slide Rd. The car went West on 50th St. from Slide Rd., and Officer Caddell stopped it on 50th St. just East of Bangor Ave. As the subject was stopping the car, Officer Caddell noticed that the door on the driver's side was partially open. As Officer Caddell walked up to the car, the subject opened the door and put his left hand on the door and his right hand on the steering wheel. Officer Caddell told the subject to step out of the car and not to make any quick motions. The subject said, "You had better move back or I will hurt you." At this time, the subject reached down into the seat with his right hand. Officer Caddell stepped behind the car and drew his pistol. The subject started to close the door of the car and said, "I don't want to be taken." Officer Caddell could not hear the last word for sure, but he thinks the last word was "alive." The subject took off at a high rate of speed, turned North on Bangor. Officer Caddell fired two shots at the Pontiac trying to disable the car. One shot struck the right rear of the car about 6″ in front of the tire. We were not able to determine where the second shot hit. The subject went North on Bangor and to 48th St. and west on 48th to Chicago

LUBBOCK AVALANCHE-JOURNAL

EVENING

VOL. 44, NO. 133 — 50 Pages — Lubbock, Texas, Wednesday Evening, March 13, 1968 — Full Leased Wires: (AP), (UPI)

BENJAMIN LACH NABBED AFTER CHASE

Student Charged In Slaying

'Liberation Army' May Invade North

Guerrilla Action Is Planned

Saigon Action Surprises U.S.

WORK BY DAVE KNAPP

Police Credit A-J With Break In Case

Stakeout At Tech Office Pays Off

Graduate Pupil Is Accused In Murder Of Woman Custodian

By DAVE KNAPP, BILL BIRGE And JOE HITCHCOCK
Avalanche-Journal Staff

Dist. Atty. Alton Griffin today charged a Texas Tech graduate student, Benjamin Lach, with murder with malice in the death of Tech custodian Sarah Alice Morgan.

Griffin said that Lach, 23, made an oral statement in regard to the Dec. 4 murder in the Tech Science building.

The charge was filed with Justice Wayne LeCroy.

Lach was arraigned at 1:45 p.m. and Judge LeCroy appointed attorney Bill Gillespie to represent him. Defense counsel's request for bond was denied and Lach was lodged in Lubbock County Jail.

Information developed by the Avalanche-Journal and later turned over to Griffin on Feb. 7 led to the apprehension of Lach, whose parents live in Mattapan, Mass., a Boston suburb.

A reward of $5,000, posted by the five banks of Lubbock, has been offered for information leading to the arrest and conviction of the person or persons responsible for the murder of Mrs. Morgan, 34.

City police, alerted by a Texas Tech professor, today set the trap which led to Lach's arrest.

Office Near Murder Scene

Suspect Leaves Master Key

Jet Crash Kills Six

DAVE KNAPP

Front-page headlines of the *Lubbock Avalanche-Journal* on the day following the arrest of Benjamin Lach for the murder of Sarah Alice Morgan. (*Lubbock Avalanche-Journal* morgue file collection, the Southwest Collection.)

where he ran a stop sign. The subject was traveling at a very high rate of speed. He continued West on 48th St. and then on a dirt road to Loop 289 and then North on Loop 289. At this point, Officer [Bill] Bailey got in behind the subject and his speed increased to 100 miles per hour plus. He continued North across Thirty-Fourth St. At this time, Officer Emerine blocked Loop 289 at the 19th St. overpass. The subject then turned East on the access road to 19th St., turned North in direction of Rest Haven Cemetary [*sic*]. He drove across graves. The car almost hit a covering over a new grave and skid around and came to rest against the rope covering of the new grave. The subject

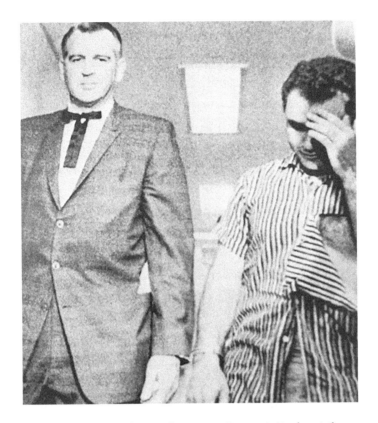

Lubbock Police Chief J. T. Alley escorts Benjamin Lach to jail shortly after the suspect was arrested in a Lubbock cemetery. (Courtesy 1968 *La Ventana* yearbook, author collection.)

jumped out of the car and started running East. Officer Bailey got out of his car with his shotgun and caught up with the subject close to the Mausoleum vault. Officer Bailey told the subject to stop and place his hands on the wall of the mausoleum which he did. But the subject had to be told several times to keep his hands on the building as he contended that he wanted to take them off and turn around. At this time, Officer Bailey put the handcuffs on the subject, and Officer Caddell and Emerine arrived along with Officers Lt. Price, Roberts, Ewing, Mowrey, Davidson, Sgt. Brewer, Chief Alley and Officer Mitchell. The subject was placed in the paddy wagon and brought to the PD by Officer Carter. The

1965 Pontiac was picked up by Rainbow Wrecker and was stored by Rainbow Wrecker.

On March 13, 1968, Benjamin Lach was charged with murder with malice, i.e., capital murder, in connection with the death of Sarah Alice Morgan, and remained in the Lubbock County Jail without bail. Wearing a torn blue-gray-striped shirt and corduroy trousers, he appeared for arraignment in front of Lubbock County Justice of the Peace Wayne LeCroy. The JP appointed Lubbock attorney William J. "Bill" Gillespie to represent Lach at an examining trial.

On the day of his apprehension, Lach gave a three-page statement to authorities implicating his involvement in the murder.

As one would expect, the arrest resulted in immense relief for Tech students and the community, as this March 14 *University Daily* article and editorial stated:

> "Techsans surprised at capture, think police bungled Morgan case"
> Lane Arthur, Copy Editor
> Techsans and their parents will sleep easier tonight with the capture of Benjamin Lach, accused killer of Mrs. Sarah Alice Morgan. No longer will Techsans be afraid to walk alone on the campus at night. No longer will students place ironing boards and bottles in front of their locked doors and sleep with a flashlight or knife nearby.
>
> A feeling of surprise and relief has spread over the campus like a comforting blanket. Dede Armentrout, who works in the lab room where Mrs. Morgan was killed, was relieved when Lach was arrested. Miss Armentrout works in the day, but not at night.
>
> "Usually there is a lot of noise outside and it's not too bad, but on Sunday afternoons it's rather quiet and it gets pretty spooky up here," she said.
>
> Miss Armentrout knew Lach but had never spoken to him.
>
> "From what I've heard, Lach has been a prime suspect for some

time, so I was not too surprised to hear they had caught him," Miss Armentrout said.

"I just can't believe they've really caught him," said Gary "Nick" Nichelson, an off-campus student. "I'm relieved. I was a little scared right after the murder when I had to take quizzes at night in the Science Building," he said.

Nichelson was also worried about girls he knew who had to go places at night. He took them himself, he said. Nichelson voiced the opinion prevalent on the campus today that the police had bungled the case.

One woman, who asked not to be identified, said she couldn't believe he would have walked into a room with two policemen and still escape.

"It's ridiculous that it took the police this long to catch him," said Toni Turpen, a freshman from Lubbock. She said girls were afraid to go to night classes and everyone was leery of the Science Building.

"After this, I'll still be afraid to walk on campus at night," Miss Turpen said.

Pat Tennison, who had a class in the Science Building Wednesday morning, said the police wouldn't let the students in but showed them pictures of the alleged killer.

"I had never seen him," she said.

Miss Tennison said she thought the police would never catch him and wondered how he ever got out of the building with all those policemen there.

"I was scared at first and my parents wouldn't let me come on the campus alone at night after the murder. I'm not scared now, though," she said.

Debbie Banks, a sophomore from Hereford, said she thought it was a stroke of luck the police ever caught him.

"Just thinking there was someone who had tried to cut a person's head off was probably somewhere on campus made me afraid to walk anywhere alone," Miss Banks said. "All the girls locked their doors at night and some of them even carried flashlights to bed with them. The wing was frightened at night when someone would walk up and down the hall and then leave," she said.

Susan Swaim, a Doak resident, thought the police did a "lousy job" handling the case. "When I heard the news this morning, I thought it was an unusual way to catch a murderer," she said.

Judy Wilson, who has kept a Girl Scout knife hidden in her room ever since the murder, said she was glad it was all over. "I was suspicious of everyone for awhile," she said.

Richard Ramsey, a senior, thought many parents would be relieved. "Every time I went home all my parents wanted to know was information about the Morgan case," Ramsey said.

Dr. Earl G. Camp, chairman of the biology department, said, "It's quite a relief that this thing has been solved. Our people have been kind of scared since the murder. Always before we had felt perfectly safe to come and go at any hour of the day or night, but the murder changed all that."

Mrs. Pearlene Glasrud, who had Lach in one of her classes, was astonished when she heard the news he had been accused of the murder. "I never dreamed it could have been one of my students," she said.

J. W. Jackson, a professor in the government department, thought Lach's apprehension would help Tech's image. "I've talked with persons in other parts of the state who were afraid to send their daughters to Tech after Mrs. Morgan was killed," Jackson said.

University Daily Editorial, March 14, 1968
"Law Enforcement Difficult Business"
The arrest of a prime suspect in the slaying of a Tech custodian will do much to relieve campus tension which has held on now since the murder more than three months ago.

As Traffic-Security Chief Bill Daniels, whose department played a significant role in the capture of the suspect, put it: "I've never been so relieved in my life!"

CHECKING NOTES — Sgt. J. D. Fortner and Chief Bill Daniels of Texas Tech security compare notes after the arrest of a suspect in a bizarre campus murder Dec. 4. Their close cooperation in the slaying probe greatly aided its progress and was instrumental in leading to the arrest of a graduate student, charged with murder with malice. (Staff Photo by Pauline Warner)

Sgt. J. D. Fortner and Chief Bill Daniels of the Texas Tech Security Office review case notes after the arrest of a suspect in the murder of Sarah Alice Morgan. (*Lubbock Avalanche-Journal* morgue file collection, the Southwest Collection.)

Of course, the immediate fear which hit the campus largely disappeared after the Christmas holidays, but queasy feelings while walking alone on campus at night or glancing at the third floor of the

Science Building have remained. Even now, they will not disappear completely.

The approximate $20,000 spent on additional security for the campus immediately following the murder now seems unneeded, but it was money well spent. It helped return a disrupted university—which Texas Tech was—to near normal. The force of fear is indeed strange and awesome.

The arrest should also restore confidence in the Lubbock Police Department, which has been privately criticized for its handling of the case and its constant "no new leads" statements.

Unquestionably, law enforcement is a difficult business and, involving one's personal security, it is easy to criticize. Oftentimes it should be criticized. But, as this case apparently has shown, it should also be remembered that law enforcement is not a job for the impatient, nor should it be judged by the impatient.

Whether the man now charged with the crime is guilty or not remains for the jury to decide, but simply for the jury to have something to decide lightens a person's apprehensions. And even then the scar remains.

"A lot of the girls on campus were scared to death [immediately after the murder]," Detective Hargrave remembered, while discussing the case years later. "Ben [Lach] was one of the guys who volunteered to walk the girls to their cars [for safety reasons]."

Benjamin Lach's unauthorized presence in Dr. Rylander's office was in itself a violation of university policy, as outlined in the 1967–1968 Texas Tech catalog:

Cheating
Dishonesty of any kind on examinations and quizzes or on written assignments, illegal possession of examinations, the use of unauthorized notes during an examination or quiz, obtaining information during an examination from the examination paper or otherwise

from another student, assisting others to cheat, alteration of grade records, illegal entry or unauthorized presence in an office are instances of cheating.

Complete honesty is required of the student in the presentation of any and all phases of course work as his own. This applies to quizzes of whatever length as well as to final examinations, to daily reports, and to term papers.

SIDEBAR: A CASE OF MIND CONTROL?

(Used with permission)

José Silva (1914–1999), an electronics repairman, developed an interest in psychology to see if it could help him increase his children's IQ. After experimenting and being convinced of his daughter's sudden clairvoyance, Silva decided to learn more about the development of psychic abilities.

In 1944, Silva began developing his method: Silva Mind Control. He used it on his family members and friends before launching it commercially in the 1960s.

Silva wrote the following article on his company's website, in which he claimed to be involved in the Alice Morgan murder investigation.

A Texas Murder Case

by José Silva

We had started to teach on a regular basis in a certain city in Texas when we became aware that the chairman of the department of psychology of the local college (it is now a university) was interested in bringing his psychology class to observe our work and comment on it. This they did.

Later, a woman who worked as a janitor at the college was murdered in a laboratory at the college, and after several months of investigation, the police had no clues to go on. One Monday morning, after we had finished training a group and were packing to move on to another city to train another group, two gentlemen came to talk to us. They were in charge of the detective division of the police department in that city. These men had been told by the head of the department of psychology that perhaps we could help in finding clues that they could use in their investigation. The officers wanted to know if this was possible. I said, "Yes, it is. A clairvoyant, from his clairvoyant level, can regress in time and can know how the person was killed and can describe the murderer. Sometimes the progress is easier when we have a piece of clothing from either the victim or the murderer," I explained. "The clairvoyant just holds the piece of clothing in his hand while getting the information."

The officers asked, "Will you do it for us?" I answered, "No." They wanted to know why, and I said, "Because we have sworn that we will never use our system to hurt anybody under any circumstances. If I help you to capture [the perpetrator], you are going to hurt him and that would be our using our system for hurting a human being."

The officers then said, "We feel it is your obligation towards society as much as it is ours to capture this criminal and keep him from hurting others. Besides, he may be sick and in need of help himself. If this is the case, he will be sent to a hospital for treatment and that would stop him from hurting others."

"I understand what you are saying," I replied, "but that is your duty, to capture criminals, and our duty is to train people to develop clairvoyance. How you use it depends on your duties."

The police officers then said, "You mean to tell us that you would teach us clairvoyance so then we, ourselves, could use clairvoyance to capture criminals?"

I answered, "What you do with it is up to you."

"Well, train us," they said. "How much will it cost?"

I said, "For you to use it for that purpose, we will do it free of charge."

"We are ready, then," they answered quickly. I then said, "We will be back one month from today to teach another group. You can then be trained."

They said, "We would like to be trained now."

I said, "Right now, that is impossible. If you had come this past weekend, you would have been trained in the first part of the training. There are four parts to the total training and in this city, we teach a part each month. In other cities, we start on a Monday night and teach every week night and all day Saturday and Sunday and that way we complete the full training in seven days. But the way we do it in this city, it would take four months."

"We can't wait that long," the officers answered. "Is there any other way of doing it?"

I said, "Yes, by following us around from city to city until you complete your training."

They said they could not do that either. They were about to leave when one said, "Is there any other way that you could help us?"

I said, "Yes."

They wanted to know how. "By presenting the case to High Intelligence," I said. At that point, they looked at each other. I could detect a confused appearance on their faces, and one said, "You mean like God?"

I said, "Yes." Again they looked at each other, still appearing confused. Then one said, "And how long do we have to wait for that?"

"Three days," I said. Both officers said at the same time, "Three days?" I said, "Yes, three days." They appeared more confused than ever, and with a tone in their voices as though they were talking to a crank or a loonie, they then said, "Let us think about it and we will let you know later. All right?"

I said that was all right, and they departed. We kept on going and meeting with our obligations to continue training other groups in other cities.

One month later we returned on a Monday to the city where the murder had taken place. In our hotel mail box was a large envelope with pictures of the murdered person in the university laboratory, and a campus map indicating the building where the murder had taken place. Along with the pictures and the map was a note saying, "Please do whatever you can to help us." Although there were no signatures on the note, we knew where it came from.

That night, I presented the case to High Intelligence. The only cases we present to High Intelligence are cases that do not respond to any other method used for the correction of problems, and cases that we do not want to participate in or be biased on. We consider High Intelligence to be that entity who has problem solving ability.

For example, if a person has the answer to one of my problems and I do not have the answer, that person is situated at a higher level of intelligence than I am, concerning that kind of problem. I may be situated at a higher level of intelligence than that same person with regard to a different kind of problem. Whoever has more answers to problems would be situated at a higher and higher level of intelligence; only God is situated at the highest level of intelligence, because God can solve all problems . . .

I have developed, through practice, a method that appears to work better when one wants to present a case to higher levels of intelligence who govern our galaxy. The method is: At night, just before retiring, you enter the clairvoyant level and program yourself to awaken at the precise time when it is your turn to present your case. Stay at your level and go to sleep from your level. When you wake up automatically, you are to reenter your level and bow your head and then mentally explain everything you know about the project, taking for granted that some higher intelligence is listening.

When presenting a case to High Intelligence, it helps to imagine that High Intelligence is behind you up in the direction of the sky, which means about twenty degrees back from your vertical position.

Besides explaining everything you know about the case, also explain what you think should be done. After you have done this, add mentally, "May the best thing happen for everybody concerned," and let the project go. Do not try to help solve it after that because you end up with it again. You have transferred the case into better hands, so let it go.

I have observed, while working hundreds of cases, that I have gotten better results when I present the case with my head lowered as in prayer. To me, it seemed that if I did not lower my head, that I would not register my tries, and if I did not try to solve the problem on my own before asking for help, I would not get help. When I tried, and tried again, and could not solve the problem, then and only then would I be entitled to get help from High Intelligence, if I had registered my tries; that is, if I tried with my head lowered. If I tried to solve a case with my head straight up, it did not matter how many times I tried, when I asked for help I would not get it.

In straightforward language, it appears that we register on a meter our tries when we try with your head lowered, and we would not register our tries with your head straight up. Then it seems that when we ask for help, some High Intelligence comes along and before helping, the intelligence looks at the meter; if tries have not been registered, we don't get help.

It also appears that we develop a reputation as to whether we are dependable or not. When we sincerely desire to help and we always do our best, we seem to establish a reputation indicating that we are dependable. A dependable person who has established a reputation will get help without having to register his tries.

The lowering of the head when working cases, I call "Aligning ourselves with the center of our galaxy." This is what I did and how I worked, or presented the murder case on that Monday night.

That same night, or early in the morning of the following day, someone entered the office of one of the professors at the college. Investigators theorized it was to find answers to test questions. A detective was assigned to watch the building the next night to see if that individual would enter again. Sure enough the individual entered the same office again. When the detective tried to capture him, the suspect escaped on a bicycle, through the buildings and pathways. He had a car parked close by, and when he reached his car he threw the bicycle in the trunk and fled in the car. Police cars were notified by radio and gave chase. They captured the fugitive on the edge of town.

This person had on him a master key that he used to enter the professor's office. The master key had belonged to the janitor woman who was murdered in the laboratory of the college. When he was questioned, the suspect confessed to the murder, and later he was convicted of the crime.

It took almost thirty-six hours after the case was presented to High Intelligence. The police investigators thought it had been a coincidence, and we agreed. For us, a "coincidence" is an act of God, and we believe that we present the cases in this manner to a department of God.

To this day, the police believe that we had nothing to do in the case, that what happened was going to happen anyway, with or without us. Our experience indicates that when we present cases in this manner, if we present the case correctly and if the case merits solution, it will always happen within 72 hours. High Intelligence chose to solve this case.

SIDEBAR: WALTER WHITAKER AND THE 1953 LUBBOCK MURDER

About fourteen years before Alice Morgan was killed, Lubbock experienced another brutal crime of violence that grabbed more headlines than any previous murder case. In 1953, Joyce Fern White, eighteen, was reported missing by her mother on January 7. Her boyfriend, Walter E. Whitaker Jr., joined in a fruitless search for the girl, suggesting she may have run away to San Antonio.

Whitaker, a twenty-year-old airman at Reese Air Force Base in Lubbock, was the well-educated son of a wealthy Connecticut industrialist. He possessed an IQ of 135 and spoke Greek and Hebrew, among other languages. Whitaker met White at Lawson's Roller Skating Rink in August 1952. Romance blossomed, and by January 1953 the couple was discussing marriage.

When notified of his transfer to San Antonio as a flying cadet, Whitaker bid goodbye to White. The girl insisted the two should marry, but he refused. Then, White informed the airman she was pregnant.

Convinced of her pregnancy, he agreed to immediately take her to Clovis, New Mexico, to marry. On the way, they stopped to make love. Afterward, she informed him she was not pregnant, and an argument ensued about his relationship with a former girlfriend.

Whitaker said White slapped him, and the next thing he remembered was looking down and seeing her discolored face. White was dead.

Eventually, police questioned him. After requesting counsel from a Lutheran minister, Whitaker led officers to the spot where he buried the girl's body.

"He took a shovel and dug six different holes, five of which produced the clothing . . . and finally . . . he dug down about four to six feet and there they found the body of Joyce Fern," according to court documents.

Whitaker was indicted for "murder with malice," a capital crime, and the ensuing legal drama was unprecedented in Lubbock's history. Relentless media coverage, highly prejudicial to Whitaker, resulted in the case being transferred to Wilbarger County on a change of venue.

A respected judge presided, and notable lawyers on both sides of the case were involved, but the trial assumed a circus atmosphere. Photographers captured dramatic events in and out of the courtroom, and the defendant, Whitaker, seemed to relish the publicity. Three days of jury selection produced twelve male jurors.

Whitaker testified, claiming what amounted to an "amnesia" defense. It did not work. The prosecution proved he purchased cotton cord shortly before White's death, and blood-stained cord was found with her corpse. White had been strangled. Following three days of testimony, jurors convicted Whitaker and sentenced him to death. After the rejection of Whitaker's appeals, he was electrocuted in Huntsville on September 1, 1954.

Whitaker's execution was Lubbock's first, and now Benjamin Lach faced the prospect of being the second Lubbock murder defendant to face Old Sparky, Texas's fabled electric chair.

CHAPTER 4

WHO IS BENJAMIN LACH?

JEOPARDY! IS A POPULAR TV GAME SHOW THAT originated in the 1960s and continues to this day, offering a unique twist: Three contestants are given an answer and then must reply with the correct question, in the form of "Who/What Is —?"

But the events in Lubbock, Texas, surrounding the murder of Alice Morgan most certainly did not rank as trivial as a television game show.

With that being said, the arrest did beg the question: Just who is Benjamin Lach, and why is he considered a suspect in the murder of Alice Morgan?

The answer was, in a word, complex.

Benjamin Lach (Lach means "laugh" in German) was a twenty-three-year-old Texas Tech student who stood five foot eight and weighed 175 pounds, with brown eyes and curly brown hair. He was

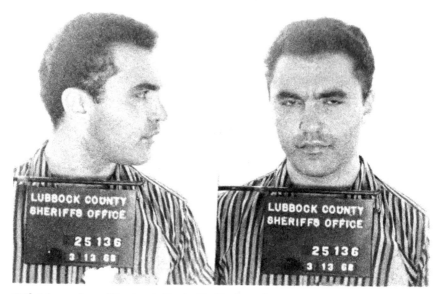

Official mugshot of Benjamin Lach. (*Lubbock Avalanche-Journal* morgue file collection, the Southwest Collection.)

born on December 10, 1944, in Bialystok, Poland, the son of Herman and Lucy Lach.

Nazis imprisoned Herman Lach in a concentration camp for a time in Poland, and his parents and seven brothers and sisters were exterminated by the Nazis. Lucy Lach also lost her parents and three siblings in death camps.

Growing up in a Jewish family at that time, young Ben had anything but an idyllic childhood. Prior to immigrating to the United States in 1958, the Lachs lived in Poland and then Israel. Because of Poland's sentiment towards Jewish people, the Lach family hid their identity. Benjamin attended a Catholic preschool and in his early years was raised solely by his mother until his father escaped the concentration camp and rejoined the family.

Benjamin was five when the family fled to Israel in 1950, where he performed well in school, learning both Hebrew and Spanish. His siblings were born there, with big brother Benjamin playfully carting his sister around in a wagon, while making cardboard puzzles for his brother, whom he called a genius.

In 1958, Herman, seeking an opportunity for a better life and sponsored by a family member, decided to move the family to Memphis, Tennessee. Not everyone looked forward to the move. Benjamin, thirteen at the time, did not want to leave the comfort of Israel for an unknown land.

The family lived in a poor section of Memphis as Benjamin struggled with his studies in school. He excelled in math but was below average in reading. Benjamin had grown up speaking Russian, Yiddish, Polish, Hebrew, and Spanish, but had never learned English. Upon entering school in Memphis he was immediately placed in two English classes. He was also the only Jewish member of the school's football team.

A year later, Herman heard about a union of Jewish bakers in Boston and the family packed up and moved to Malden, Massachusetts. There, Benjamin attended a highly diverse high school that included Jewish, Irish, Italian, and Catholic students. After graduating from Malden High School, he suffered a neck injury in a car accident in Malden in 1965.

Lach attended summer school at Harvard University in 1966, then studied at Boston University (leaving after one semester due to poor grades) and Lincoln University (a predominantly Black institution in Pennsylvania) before eventually graduating from Suffolk University (Boston) in June 1967 with a bachelor of arts degree in chemistry.

Lach was one of thirty-two bachelor of arts degree graduates listed in the Suffolk commencement program dated September 24, 1967. Commencement exercises were held at 3 p.m. in the Suffolk University Auditorium with Sen. Claiborne Pell of Rhode Island offering remarks.

According to the 1967 Suffolk University yearbook, Lach was a member of the Psychology Club and the Science Club, a math tutor, and a physical science instructor.

At the time of Lach's arrest, his father, working as a baker, resided in Mattapan (near Boston), Massachusetts, with wife Lucy and Benjamin's brother (age eleven) and sister (age fourteen).

CANDIDATES FOR THE DEGREE OF BACHELOR OF ARTS
CUM LAUDE

CHARLES K. BUTLER, JR.	Roslindale	DAVID ALBAN REIS	Weymouth
WILLIAM DENNIS MURRAY	Brockton	KAREN ANN SPANEAS	Arlington
	LEON J. TOUSIGNANT	Dedham, Mass.	

CANDIDATES FOR THE DEGREE OF BACHELOR OF ARTS

PETER F. AINSWORTH	Brighton	JAMES E. KEOGH	Methuen
RICHARD LEONARD ANDERSON	Bradford	BENJAMIN LACH	Mattapan
JOHN W. BEAN	West Roxbury	BARRY R. LATZMAN	Brooklyn, New York
GEOFFREY RHODES BIRD	Boston	PAUL CHARLES MAGWOOD	Dorchester
STEPHEN THEODORE CAPARELL	West Roxbury	PAUL V. McCAFFREY	Boston
GARY P. CASTANINO	Waltham	JOHN EDWIN McCARTHY	Milton
NICHOLAS CATOGGIO, JR.	East Boston	PHILIP JOSEPH McCARTHY	Arlington
LEONARD LANDON DAVIS III	Boston	BRIAN ROBERT MERRICK	Brookline
JOSEPH LOUIS ESPOSITO, JR.	Braintree Highlands	DAVID A. O'BRIEN	Cambridge
JOHN C. FISHER	Worcester	VINCENT deP. O'SULLIVAN	Dorchester
MICHAEL WARREN FOSTER	Boston	MARIE E. TRAHAN PEPE	Medford
DANIEL J. HARRINGTON	Belmont	JANET M. POOR	Boston
ALEXANDER AUGUSTINE HARVEY	Methuen	DENNIS PATRICK RYAN	Boston
	RALPH CLIFFORD SULLIVAN	Natick	

CANDIDATE FOR THE DEGREE OF BACHELOR OF SCIENCE
CUM LAUDE

JUDY BOND CODDING   St. Petersburg, Florida

CANDIDATES FOR THE DEGREE OF BACHELOR OF SCIENCE

WINSHIP CLEVELAND FULLER		RICHARD F. PACELLA	Revere
	Barrington, Rhode Island	FREDERICK WILLIAM RILEY	Revere
WILLIAM D. GUTERMUTH, JR.		WILLIAM ROSE	Newton
	Hoosick Falls, New York	THOMAS LOUIS SALVATORE	Derby, Connecticut
ANTHONY A. LOMBARDI	Nahant	SANDRA JEAN SAVINELLI	Lawrence
WILLIAM J. McINTYRE	Boston	GAIL L. SPICER	Cambridge

CANDIDATES FOR THE DEGREE OF
MASTER OF ARTS IN EDUCATION

JOHN J. ANSELMO, JR.	Hanover	BERTHA E. LANDMAN	Stoughton
EDWARD P. BRADY	Lynnfield	THOMAS PETERS	Mattapan
MARK LAMAR BYERS	Cambridge	STEPHEN RANDO, JR.	Waltham
ANTONIO J. A. DAMIAN	Medford	DONALD CAMERON RININGER, JR.	Boston
JUDITH M. GOLDSBERRY	Abington	GEORGE STEPHEN USEVICH	Norwood
	CALVIN WILLIAMS	Beverly Farms	

Prior to enrolling at Texas Tech, Benjamin Lach graduated from Suffolk University. (Author collection.)

Benjamin Lach arrived at Texas Tech in September 1967, seeking credits for subsequent admission to medical school in Kansas City. His 1967 fall schedule of classes at Tech follows:

Monday-Wednesday-Friday
7:30 a.m.–8:30 a.m.—Foundations of Secondary Education 330
Description: Eligibility for admission to the Teacher Education
Program. Introduction to secondary education; basic principles
underlying the secondary school program.
Location: Administration Building 313
Assistant Professor Weldon Beckner
Grade: B–
Absences: 5

8:30 a.m.–9:30 a.m.—History of the United States to 1877 231
Location: Social Science Building 113
Professor Ernest Wallace
Grade: C–
Absences: 2

10:30 a.m.–11:30 a.m.—Curriculum Development in Secondary
Education 334
Description: Foundations of curriculum development, patterns of
organization, principles and procedures, curriculum resource units,
and issues in curriculum development. Observation required.
Location: Administration Building 267
Professor Levi Nagle Jr.
Grade: B-
Absences: 1

Tuesday-Thursday-Saturday
8:30 a.m.—Comparative Vertebrate Anatomy 241
Description: Structure and evolution of the vertebrates. Laboratory
study of the anatomy of representative vertebrate types.
Location: Biology Auditorium
Assistant Professor Michael Kent Rylander
Grade: A

Absences: 0

10:30 a.m.—American Government Functions 232
Description: Government 231 and 232 or the equivalent thereof are
required of all candidates for a degree and are prerequisites to all
advanced courses.
Location: Social Science Building 112
Instructor Pearlene Vestal Glasrud
Grade: C
Absences: 2

Tuesday
1:30 p.m.–4:30 p.m.—Comparative Vertebrate Anatomy Lab 241
Description: Structure and evolution of the vertebrates. Laboratory
study of the anatomy of representative vertebrate types.
Location: Science Building 216
Assistant Professor Michael Kent Rylander
Grade: A
Absences: 0

Although busy at school, Lach also took a job at Hertz Rent-a-Car,
located at Main Street and Ave. O in downtown Lubbock in October
1967. He had moved into a basement apartment (2318 Main Street) on
September 25, 1967, and lived alone until January 31, 1968, when two
other Tech students, David Robinson and Wayne Robertson, both of
whom were seniors, took up residence there. Only a single wall separated
the three basement inhabitants.

Mr. and Mrs. F. B. Kyle owned the boardinghouse, conveniently situated just a few blocks east of Tech and a short walk to campus (and
the Science Building.)

"I don't want to say anything about him," Mrs. Kyle told the
University Daily shortly after the arrest. "He is really like a son. I was
never so shocked in my entire life. I think the world of Ben. I've never

The old F. B. Kyle boardinghouse, on Main Street near the Texas Tech campus, was where Benjamin Lach lived (in the basement) while attending Tech in 1967–1968. The house was still standing when this photo was taken in 2003 but was later demolished and is now the site of a parking lot. (Author collection.)

been afraid of him. I've been down in the basement with him many times. I'd trust him anywhere."

Mrs. Kyle added that she and Lach had talked at length about his plans to attend medical school. "He said he loved children and thought he wanted to go into pediatrics. He was supposed to go to medical school in Kansas City after he finished his work at Tech."

Robinson also expressed shock at his neighbor's arrest. "Ben was a nice guy and real witty sometimes. I liked him," Robinson said. He said Lach didn't know many people and spent most of his time studying, going to school, and working. Bowling appeared to be his only recreational hobby.

Robinson's fiancée, Lynda Everitt, seemed equally stunned at the news of Lach's arrest. "I really liked Ben, he was so nice," she said. "I even mentioned the murder to him. I asked him if he had been here first semester and had known about our famous murder. He just said 'yes' and that's all."

Friends described Lach as a "quiet, lone-wolf type" who often cooked his own meals to save money.

According to Robinson, Everitt had recently set up a date for Lach with one of her friends. Lach commented that this was one of the first dates that he had since coming to Texas.

"Lach worked at the Hertz Rent-a-Car place as a maintenance man, keeping the cars cleaned up and the like," Robinson said. "He had been working about forty hours a week but this was interfering with his school work so he started putting in about twenty. He would go to work about 5 a.m. and come in around 7 p.m. or 8 p.m. He would generally stay home after he got home from work, you know, studies and all. He was taking a full load, either twelve or fourteen hours."

T. C. Douglass, the personnel manager at Hertz, painted a slightly different picture of Lach the employee. "[He was] a peculiar boy, a little odd, and not particularly friendly," Douglass said. "He was moody, but we never had any indication of his acting violent. He didn't have much to do with the other workers; he was a loner." Douglass said that Lach was difficult to talk to, but "this could have just been due to his accent and his not being from this part of the country.

"Lach was not what I would call a good worker," Douglass said. "We started once to let him go but kept him because he needed the money."

Company time cards revealed that Lach did not report to work on the day of the murder: December 4, 1967.

Lach told his two housemates that he decided to enroll at Texas Tech because he needed one course to gain admission into medical school. When Suffolk University in Boston informed him that he needed the course, it was too late to register for the class at any college other than Tech on account of its relatively late registration time (September 18–23).

In addition to being basement neighbors, Robinson and Lach both just happened to be in Dr. Rylander's embryology class in the spring of 1968. According to Robinson, the night before Lach's arrest on

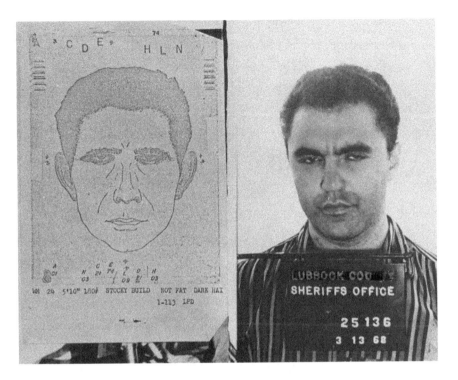

(left) Composite drawing of an individual authorities were seeking to question in the murder of Alice Morgan. (right) Mug shot of Benjamin Lach. (*Lubbock Avalanche-Journal* morgue file collection, the Southwest Collection.)

March 13, the two had studied together for Rylander's Wednesday quiz. "Ben seemed to know the material pretty well," Robinson said. "He answered several questions for me."

Shortly after the arrest, Rylander described in detail the scenario that led to the stakeout of his office to the *University Daily*:

> Lach had been a prime suspect since the murder last December because of his resemblance to a general description of a man seen talking to Mrs. Morgan on the night of the murder.
>
> Other members of the faculty were suspicious of Lach, but this whole thing started with me last Monday when Miss [Barbara] White [junior anthropology major and part-time secretary of New Deal] typed a stencil for an embryology 332 quiz I was to give at 5:30 p.m.

Wednesday.

She intended to run it off Tuesday, so Monday evening I put the stencil in the bottom drawer of my file cabinet. I had suspected someone had been coming in my office [room 324 of the Science Building] and looking in my file cabinet, so I stuck a little piece of paper in the cabinet lock.

If I found the piece of paper had dropped out of the lock, I would know that someone had been tampering with the cabinet.

I had classes from 7:30 to 9:30 Tuesday morning and came by my office about 7:25 to pick up my lecture notes. The piece of paper was still there just where I had stuck it, so nobody had tampered with the filing cabinet Monday night.

Ben [Lach] was in my 7:30 embryology class, but he didn't show up until about 8. Meanwhile, Miss White had come by the office about 8:10 and noticed the piece of paper had flipped down onto my desk.

This could mean that Lach entered the office any time between 7:25 and 8:10 with plenty of time to open the file cabinet and look at the quiz stencil.

I returned to my office at 9:30 and noticed the piece of paper on my desk. Up to this point, both Miss White and I thought the other one had opened the file cabinet.

But then we saw each other about noon and discovered that neither of us had touched the file case. It was then that I notified campus Traffic-Security, and an officer came over in just a few minutes.

I typed a report of the incident and asked the officer to take the quiz stencil so it could be checked for fingerprints.

I understand that the Lubbock police and the district attorney's office were called into the case at that point, and the police staked out my office Tuesday night.

You see, I felt whoever had come into my office Tuesday [had to] come back because the original stencil contained only 31 questions of a 50-question test. So if Ben saw the quiz Tuesday morning he would be able to do well on only three-fifths of it. He would have to see the remaining 19 questions in order to do well throughout the test.

The quiz itself was optional. I had seen Ben on Monday and asked him if he planned to take it. He seemed very defensive at that time.

He had not taken the last optional quiz.

There was nothing missing from my file cabinet, but a large pair of paper scissors is missing from my office. I don't know if Ben took them or not.

In 2004, during an oral history interview with the Texas Tech Special Collections Library, Rylander said Lach was "actually, as a person, very likable, very intellectual. And he would come in and talk to me sometimes about all sorts of intellectual things, you know. He had an inquiring mind. He really wanted to be a doctor."

Another one of the 150 students in Rylander's comparative anatomy class was Don Bridgers, a tall, reserved, mild-mannered geology major and biology minor. He recalled that at the time of the Morgan slaying, he and other students were on a field trip to the Gulf Coast. When they returned to campus, the Science Building was under heavy security, and he talked to two police officers one night while he was in a class. Although they were fellow students in Rylander's anatomy class, Lach and Bridgers were not acquainted. Bridgers earned his degree in 1968 and joined the Lubbock police force in October of that year. From 1990 to 1993, he served as Lubbock Police Chief.

Larry Hagood, a farmer and real estate businessman who lived a few miles from Lubbock, near Tahoka, Texas, was another acquaintance of Lach who expressed shock at news of the arrest.

"He spent Thanksgiving with us and had visited in our home since then," Hagood told the *A-J*. Lach had been invited to spend the holiday with the Hagoods in Tahoka because Mrs. Hagood, who befriended him while seated next to him in Professor Levi Nagle's Secondary Education 334 class, knew he was a long way from home and would be lonely over the holidays. Larry Hagood said it was his understanding that Lach's

ig, March 15, 1968

MURDER SCENE—Dist. Atty. Alton R. Griffin, second from ... in a lab on the third floor of the Science Building are Lub-

Shortly after the arrest of Benjamin Lach, two Boston law enforcement officials visited Lubbock in an attempt to question him about a similar murder at Suffolk University. Shown at the scene of the Sarah Alice Morgan murder in the Texas Tech Science Building are Lubbock Police Lt. C. G. Bartley, Lubbock District Attorney Alton Griffin, Boston Police Lt. Edward Sherry, and Boston Assistant District Attorney Sal Ingenere. Lach's attorneys refused to allow the Boston officials to question their client. (*Lubbock Avalanche-Journal* morgue file collection, the Southwest Collection.)

parents had met in a German concentration camp in Poland during World War II and that his mother was "a highly educated woman." Lach, he said, indicated that she had encouraged him to make good grades and to become a doctor.

"He spent the night before Thanksgiving with us and I loaned him my car so he could go to Lubbock to work the next day," Hagood said. "Then he came back and spent the next night with us. He brought our three children some small gifts and he and I sat up late that night talking. My kids enjoyed his visits." Hagood said that on one occasion, Lach took the time to play chess with the Hagoods' twelve-year-old son.

News of Lach's arrest quickly made it to Boston, Massachusetts, where detectives showed more than a passing interest. On May 31, 1967, at Suffolk University, fifty-two-year-old nightwatchman Francis Maguire was bludgeoned to death after sulfuric acid had been thrown in his face. Maguire's keys were missing when his body was discovered in a sub-basement of a five-story building at the university. This crime occurred just six months prior to the murder of Alice Morgan.

Boston homicide Lt. Edward Sherry, who had been an investigator in the Boston Strangler case in the early 1960s, and Boston Assistant District Attorney Sal Ingenere flew to Lubbock on March 14, 1968, to confer with District Attorney Griffin and Lubbock police about similarities in the Lubbock and Boston murder cases.

"We felt Maguire might have come up on an intruder in the building," Sherry told the *A-J*. He said the acid apparently was thrown in Maguire's face in a student lounge in the basement of the building. There were also signs that his body was dragged thirty feet, down a flight of stairs and into the boiler room in the sub-basement.

Boston police theorized that the murder took place at approximately 10 p.m., although Maguire's body was not discovered until 1:30 a.m. the following day.

Lach, on the advice of his court-appointed attorney Bill Gillespie, refused to be interviewed by the Boston authorities.

"I'm surprised that we didn't get to talk to him," Ingenere said. "We wouldn't have been hanging around if we didn't think we would get a chance to ask him some questions."

Sherry was also disappointed but vowed to press forward. "There are two ways of getting evidence," Sherry said. "You get it from the lips of the suspect or you get it against him. Personally, I'd rather get it against him. We have to, we've already been prevented in getting it from him. . . . Those are the rules of the ball game and we play by the rules. Certainly, this isn't the end of the road by any means. We've got a lot of digging to do when we get back."

According to newspaper reports, prior to arriving in Lubbock, Sherry and Ingenere had determined that at the time of the Maguire murder, Lach was attending Suffolk and that he was allegedly in the building where the murder occurred on the night of the crime.

Sherry earlier revealed that Lach had been arrested on a breaking and entering charge in Wellesley, Massachusetts. At that time, Lach was surprised by police inside the home of a Harvard professor. Neighbors heard breaking glass and summoned police, who apprehended Lach. Boston police quoted Lach as saying "that he just had to get a look at his grades," as he was enrolled in a summer session at Harvard in 1966.

When all was said and done, Lach received probation for that incident.

On the day following Lach's arrest for the murder of Alice Morgan, District Attorney Griffin said that authorities had considered him the "prime suspect" for at least six weeks. Dr. Julian Biggers, acting assistant dean of the School of Education, was apparently the first person to notice the likeness between Lach and one of the composite drawings circulated shortly after the murder. Biggers told the *A-J* that he remembered speaking to Lach during registration (September 18–23) for the fall semester. (That fall, for the first time, registration was centralized and held in the Lubbock Municipal Coliseum. Prior to that, students traveled from building to building to pick up class tickets and pay their fees.) At that time, however, Biggers did not know Lach by name. He said he saw Lach again in late January when he came by to fill out forms for spring registration. On learning Lach's identity and recalling his likeness to one of the composite drawings, Biggers forwarded his suspicions to the Tech security office on January 26.

Dr. Harold Lewis, an assistant biology professor at Tech since 1965, registered Lach at the beginning of the spring semester (registration was January 29–February 3). According to Lewis, Lach not only appeared to be the man in one of the composite drawings but was also a dead ringer for a person he had seen in the north attic on the third floor of the Science Building on several occasions prior to the murder. Lewis passed this information on to the campus police.

Dave Knapp was a *Lubbock Avalanche-Journal* special assignments and police reporter in 1967. He was a key figure in working with the authorities in identifying Benjamin Lach as a murder suspect and in the subsequent stakeout of Dr. Kent Rylander's office. (*Lubbock Avalanche-Journal* morgue file collection, the Southwest Collection.)

"I didn't know Lach personally," said Dr. Earl Camp, chair of the biology department. "I saw him several times but had no real impression of him. He told me in spring registration he was a graduate student but needed undergraduate work in the biology department in order to improve his undergraduate record so he could get into medical school."

Lach indicated to Camp that he would seek teacher certification if his application to medical school was not accepted, thereby explaining his enrollment in education courses.

At the time of the murder, Lach was a student in Dr. Rylander's comparative anatomy class. Early in the fall semester, he made erratic and failing grades in the class, but his grades improved dramatically after the slaying and he completed the course with an "A."

Lach enrolled in Rylander's embryology class in the spring of 1968, and the professor hired the student to work as a lab assistant on Mondays from 1:30 p.m. to 4:30 p.m. for $1.05 an hour. One of Lach's duties included assisting with dissection under the direction of comparative anatomy instructor Kay Pittard. The lab where Lach and the students worked was on the second floor of the Science Building.

"He did work hard," Pittard said, shortly after the arrest. "He seemed conscientious about his work. I wouldn't call him quiet, either. He was really quite talkative."

A-J reporter Dave Knapp, a barrel-chested man with a silver crew cut and the look of a Marine, had been doggedly following the Morgan murder case since day one. Throughout the investigation, Knapp, morning edition editor Jay Harris, reporter Kenneth May, and other *A-J* staffers conducted more than 125 interviews with various people involved in the probe.

It was Knapp who received a confidential tip in early February that Lach might be a suspect in the case. Under the pretense of writing a feature story on the Texas Tech lab where Lach worked, Knapp and photographer Pauline Warner visited the class to take a series of photographs of the students, including the suspect.

The *A-J* gathered the photographs, along with a composite drawing produced earlier by police, and visited a number of witnesses who had seen an unidentified man in the Science Building on the night of the murder. Seven people said the photo of Lach resembled the short, stocky, wavy-haired man seen loitering in the Science Building.

Working as a paid lab assistant, Benjamin Lach (center) offers assistance to science students in the spring of 1968. (*Lubbock Avalanche-Journal* morgue file collection, the Southwest Collection.)

With this identification in hand, *A-J* morning editor Jay Harris called on one of the local law enforcement agencies, only to be told they were too busy at the time to question Lach. Harris and Knapp then forwarded the information to District Attorney Griffin, who requested the Lubbock police pick up Lach for questioning the next day.

Police did just that on February 8, transporting him to the Lubbock office of the Department of Public Safety, where he submitted to a polygraph examination and then was released.

Four days later, he went through the same routine, taking another polygraph and being released. Authorities continued to learn more about their prime suspect, as on March 4, Texas Tech clinical psychologist Dr. Murray Kovnar examined Lach. Just nine days later, on March 13, Lach was arrested at Resthaven Cemetery after fleeing from detectives in Rylander's office.

In public comments, Griffin was quick to acknowledge the role played by the *A-J* in the events, stating the information they provided "proved to be the stepping stone that led to other steps, finally resulting in the arrest."

Following the arrest, Lubbock County sheriff's deputies received numerous requests from individuals wanting to talk to Lach "about his soul" or "to bring him Bibles," but any visits were strictly regulated.

Perhaps no one grew to know Lach better than J. Blair Cherry Jr., who was a young first assistant district attorney at the time of the murder.

"Benjamin Lach was a very bright individual, and very likeable personally," Cherry said in a 2004 interview. "Once Lach was identified, the police undertook to find out as much detail of his activities here in Lubbock as they could. I was directed to check out his background . . . who he was, where he came from, prior criminal record, scholastic record, etc. . . . . His psychological makeup was very complex. . . . . Throughout the investigation, he was very cooperative. . . . I think it was almost a game to him. In the midst of the investigation, he asked us to leave him alone for a week because his girlfriend was coming to visit, and he didn't want her to know about the investigation. We did, although [District Attorney] Alton [Griffin] and I were both in the midst of election campaigns, and the newspaper knew we thought we knew who had committed the murder. But we let him have his week, then had more discussions with him."

Cherry continued: "Once we [DA's office] got involved, Alton Griffin directed the investigation. Whatever occurred after that point was largely due to his direction. He had numerous contacts with Lach throughout and coordinated with the police at every step. I can tell you that without his involvement, the case would have never been made."

"I took [Lach's] confession over at the police department that same morning of his arrest," Griffin said. "I was very careful about everything, including the Miranda Warning. . . . I felt sorry for [Lach]. In my opinion, he had a mother who demanded excellence out of him and he wasn't capable of excellence. He had an overpowering desire to please his mother. He was like a coyote—he will run from you until you get him cornered, and then he'll attack."

Butch Hargrave, one of the stakeout detectives, also became well acquainted with Lach. "I was around Ben quite a bit [after his arrest]," Hargrave said. "We searched his apartment, had some sit-down interviews with him, and I took him in for the polygraph and sodium pentothal test. Ben was a super-intelligent individual."

"[Benjamin Lach] was a pretty good kid," said Larry Hagood, whose family had befriended the college student. "When I first heard he was a suspect on the news, I couldn't believe it . . . he was the kind of person that you would take in your house in a minute. He was quiet until you got to know him, but he was very personable. And he loved children."

"You have to understand, I was 12 years old at that time [of the murder]," Larry's son Walt Hagood recalled. "So, anything that I say is from the perspective of a 12-year-old. Ben spent a lot of time with us kids [Walt and his two sisters]—he and I played chess a lot, and he brought me a model car one time. He was a stout person, very athletic and very strong. Ben was a clean-cut, well-mannered, and soft-spoken guy. I was fascinated with having a 24-year-old as a friend—someone to look up to. I just liked him."

Walt recalled the two visits that Lach made to the Hagood home—at Thanksgiving in 1967, just a couple of weeks prior to the murder of Alice Morgan, and again in early 1968, a few weeks after the murder. "On the latter visit, Ben's girlfriend came with him so Ben stayed with me in my room for a couple of nights," Walt said. "I remember him doing 100 pushups before going to bed."

In an ironic twist, Walt recalls first hearing of the murder: "We [Walt and his sisters] were in the kitchen with my mom as she was reading the newspaper [about the murder]. My mom said that the person who lifted the aquarium, the person who committed the crime, had to be very strong. And I said, 'Strong like Ben, Mom?'"

SIDEBAR: BENJAMIN LACH AND ALBERT DESALVO

Some call it a coincidence, but it's a fact: in the early 1960s, Benjamin Lach and Albert DeSalvo (aka the Boston Strangler) both resided in Malden, Massachusetts.

Malden, a working-class town located five miles north of Boston, was founded in 1857; the 1960 census showed the population to be 57,676.

Benjamin Lach graduated from Malden High School in 1963, and during that time Malden was considered a preeminent school that sent many students to Ivy League institutions.

Meanwhile, a young maintenance worker named Albert DeSalvo, his wife, and two small children also resided in Malden. And from June 1962 to January 1964, an unknown "Boston Strangler" terrorized the area, murdering thirteen women. The modus operandi was to convince the women to let him inside their homes or apartments under the pretense of maintenance or repair work. The killer then assaulted and strangled his victims. DeSalvo confessed to those heinous crimes, but he was never charged with the murders.

For earlier offenses of assault and armed robbery, the thirty-five-year-old received a life sentence in 1967. After escaping from Bridgewater State Hospital, DeSalvo was recaptured and sent to Walpole, a maximum-security prison. In 1973, he was stabbed to death at the prison, and no one was ever convicted of the crime.

In 2009, Malden ranked as the "Best Place to Raise Your Kids" in Massachusetts by *Bloomberg Businessweek* magazine. And in 2013, a study by the National Center for Education Statistics found that Malden High School was the most diverse public high school in Massachusetts. Enrollment today is approximately 1,800 students.

SIDEBAR: NATIONAL HEADLINERS CLUB HONORS *AVALANCHE-JOURNAL*

In 1969, the National Headliners Club honored the *Lubbock Avalanche-Journal* with an award for "outstanding public service" for its coverage of the

Benjamin Lach case. The award, accepted at an Atlantic City, New Jersey, luncheon by *A-J* editor and publisher Charles Guy, recognized the efforts of Dave Knapp, Jay Harris, and Kenneth May. By 1972, Knapp was executive editor, when he hired (and fired) a young reporter and Texas Tech student named Scott Pelley. Pelley would go on to a career as a national TV correspondent, serving as anchor on the *CBS Evening News* (following such legends and Texans as Walter Cronkite and Dan Rather) and on *60 Minutes*.

SIDEBAR: ALTERNATE STUDENT NEWSPAPER CRITICIZES MEDIA COVERAGE OF CASE

While the *A-J* received national plaudits for its coverage of the Benjamin Lach case, an alternative student newspaper at Tech—*The Activist Forum*—was critical of the Lubbock daily and other media outlets.

The short-lived publication (seven issues in 1968–1969 at ten cents a copy) was based on "the feeling of some students that excessive editorial restrictions in campus and local news media necessitate and justify another paper, one which can and will present a broader spectrum of facts and comments to the Tech Community."

Appearing in the *Forum*'s May 1968 issue was a lengthy article by Lillian George, titled "Until Proven Guilty," which stated, in part:

> Responsible news media reveal the truth about daily events. In criminal cases the media are obligated to maintain an atmosphere of doubt about the guilt of the accused who is "innocent until proven guilty" by courts. The arrest of Benjamin Lach with subsequent news coverage demonstrated negligence of this obligation and may have convicted Lach in the public eye.
>
> The media emphasized the ethnic element, printed part of the accused's statement prior to its acceptance as evidence, prejudiced the case by editorials, overplaying circumstantial evidence, treating it as fact, exposed Lach's criminal record, and, finally, presented parts of the DA's hypothesis for fitting the facts together.

The Activist

FORUM

Volume I Issue III 10¢ per copy Lubbock, Texas 10¢ per copy May, 1968

The Forum Presents The '68 Grover

It's that time of year again when awards, like flowers, blossom and fill with their fragrance every cranny of our otherwise empty lives. There are Oscar's and Tony's and Emmy's and Grammy's and many others. We conformists and group thinkers of the Forum staff thought it would be good for us to give some awards, for certainly there are those here who deserve awards. And, although we are generally a malcontent and cheerless lot, we rather paradoxically like to see people happy. Accordingly, with the hope that happiness will fill the lives of all those who receive awards from us, we present the 1968 Forum SPECIAL AWARDS Program, concluded by the presentation of THE 1968 GROVER.

We present the following SPECIAL AWARDS:

The GOLDEN BROOM AWARD to our Dean of Women, to give her a flying start toward retirement.

The NEW LEFT AWARD to Dean Allen for his leadership of the Student Power Revolution at Texas State University.

The BACKBONE-OF-THE-YEAR AWARD to Grover Murray, who needs one.

The OPTIMIST-OF-THE-YEAR AWARD to Librarian Janeway for his tedious and wasteful book check-out system.

The BADGE 714 AWARD to Bill Daniels of Traffic-Security for his unforgettable words "Get off them flowers!"

The MOTHER-OF-THE-YEAR AWARD (commonly called the "mother") to Guy Moore of the Housing Office for his frequent and mostly unsuccessful attempts to bring strayed children back home.

The PLATFORMATE AWARD to Dr. Kline Nall (yes, children, he does exist) of the English Dept. for the longest-dragging TV serial in Texas State University history.

The GOLDEN LION MEDALLION to Nelson Longley, Student Union Director, for his courage in selling the Forum.

The SILVER SPOON AWARD to Roy Furr for his tasteless reign as Chairman of the Board. (Roy, you're a real card. Our congratulations to you.)

The SCUM-FLOATS-TO-THE-TOP AWARD, given jointly to all incompetent faculty and administrators just now reaching "the top" through seniority and due process.

The ANONYMOUS AWARD to Dr. Gabe Kennedy, whoever that might be.

The BLIND-LEADING-THE-BLIND CITATION to graduate teaching assistants for their guts.

The STANFORD-BINET AWARD, to the Texas State Technological University Traffic-Flow Planning Commission for their placement of traffic lights near the Wiggins "Inferiority Complex" Dorms.

The UNKNOWN SOLDIER MEDAL to General Hershey, who doesn't know.

The VIRGIN CERTIFICATE to the one unnamed and unsung Freshwoman who kept her cool all year long.

To Max Blakney, in recognition of his leadership abilities, we award the MR. SMILES CITATION.

To the last and least in our SPECIAL AWARDS group goes the YELLOW TOILET ROLL SCROLL--to David Snyder and his shameless and brainless oafs at the U.D.

Now--and I know you've been waiting with considerable anticipation for this part of the awards--it is at last time for the presentation of the winner and runner-up for the GROVER. Our judges assure me that they have labored long over these choice selections. So let's all try to be partly happy with the decisions.

THE GROVER

THE GROVER, our award given for the most outstanding performance of either classical tragedy or unintentional comedy, goes to our school's Board of Directors for their consistent ability to act emotionally and irrationally in situations requiring intelligent progressive and decisive actions. We feel that their performance has best approximated the essence--the spirit--of THE GROVER.

The runnerup for THE GROVER was the majority of the student body of our school for the sensitivity, thoughtfulness, and concern among them which produced, from an enrollment in excess of 17,000, only about 4,000 who were willing to take time to vote in the Executive elections or in the recent CHOICE '68 referendum.

Page 2

Until Proven Guilty

by Lillian George

Responsible news media reveal the truth about daily events. In criminal cases the media are obligated to maintain an atmosphere of doubt about the guilt of the accused who is 'innocent until proven guilty' by courts. The arrest of Benjamin Lach with subsequent news coverage demonstrated negligence of this obligation and may have convicted Lach in the public eye.

The media emphasized the ethnic element, printed parts of the accused's statement prior to its acceptance as evidence, prejudiced the case by editorials, overplayed circumstantial evidence, treating it as fact, exposed Lach's criminal record, and, finally, presented parts of the DA's hypothesis for fitting the facts together.

Local radio broadcasts hammered "foreign student" into the public's ear, failing to mention on several occasions his naturalized citizenship. Lubbock's A-J emphasized "Polish born" in the March 15 morning edition. Radio station KSEL however, did editorially castigate other news services for their handling of the case.

Parts of Lach's three - page statement were published in the A-J March 14 morning edition. Appearing on the front page under the headline "Student Gives DA Statement" was the following, "Although contents of the subject's statement were not publicly disclosed, the Avalanche-Journal learned that Lach had indicated Mrs. Morgan surprised him in room 304-J...." Treating a statement of questionable validity (from a second-hand source) as a fact is considered poor journalism, but to print part of the accused's statement before it is accepted as evidence in the case can be illegal although in this case it is within the letter (only) of the law since no quotations are from the statement itself. Newspapers are also prohibited from calling a statement a confession before it is accepted as such in court. Radio and television stations don't seem to be held by the same law, though, for many actually said Lach confessed. Later at the examining trial, Justice of the Peace Wayne LeCroy did accept Lach's statement as evidence, so any suits that could have resulted from these loose observances of the law were nullified. But one must ask this: Should one obey a law only to protect himself, or to prevent injury to others?

Two questionable editorials appeared in the University Daily. One was in the Thursday March 14 edition, under the title "Law Enforcement Difficult Business." The writer quotes Traffic-Security chief Bill Daniels as saying "I've never been so relieved in my life" about the capture of Lach. And, another paragraph down, the writer states, "The approximate $20,000 spent on additional security for the campus immediately following the murder now seems unnecessary...." By the time the last paragraph says "If the man now charged with the crime is guilty or not is for the jury to decide," the damage is done. It is already stated in so many words that we can all rest easy because the killer is caught.

Roy McQueen's editorial, "Who'll Get Reward" in the Friday March 15 issue of the UD is the other questionable editorial. The author seems convinced that the case is broken, that the killer is caught and that the only thing left to do is to decide who should get the reward.

These UD articles can be excused fairly easily as the products of inexperienced criminal reporting. However, the staffs of the professional news services know (we hope) laws regarding criminal reporting and thus should receive no quarter.

Overplaying sensational circumstantial evidence and treating it as conclusive was more widespread than any other offense. In the March 13 evening edition on p. 14-A, the A-J stated that reporters obtained "positive identification from at least seven persons" that Lach was the same man seen loitering around the Science Building. But they failed to mention the time element: these identifications were obtained more than a month following the incident.

See: Lach (Cont. on page 8)

THE PLAYPEN

During the past year, the Board of Directors have been confronted by the need to make several policy decisions. They have also had before them for well over a year the Name Change. And on February 10 of this year, the Board finally acted: it passed a resolution limiting freedom of speech and thought on this campus. Quite a record..........

The first issue of the Forum advocated a reversal of this anti-free-speech resolution. The Board failed even to consider this request. Recently it has become clear that the resolution is also in violation of AAUP principles. Will our Board always wait until it is forced to change--like a child with soiled breeches who isn't ready to quit playing? Or will it begin to act responsibly and on its own initiative? Board, we are waiting. Who will change your underwear this time--you, or someone else?

While we recognize the need for honest deliberation in making changes, we are tired of your deliberate evasion of responsibility on the Name Change. It is apparent that Texas State University is the name most favored, even among exes. Yet you still procrastinate, waiting no doubt for an Act of the Olympians from whose decisions there is little appeal. We know that you are all very busy, very important people (we hesitate to say "men"), but you must consider yourselves far more important than the degree candidates of this school, more important than the future of this school.

Frankly, we don't think you are.

The Activist Forum—a short-lived alternative student newspaper—criticized local media coverage after the arrest of Benjamin Lach. (Courtesy the Southwest Collection, *The Activist Forum* 1, no. 3.)

The article went on to specifically criticize the *Avalanche-Journal* and *University Daily* for biased coverage.

However, George's article concludes with a somewhat softer view of the coverage:

> The newspaper articles and radio and TV broadcasts revealing the facts about the arrest of and case against the suspect were in most cases in strict accordance with the law. Opinions were given in quotations, as were any statements of questionable validity. However, the spirit of the law—a true concern for keeping the minds of the public open—was absent from all but a few of the news media.

CHAPTER 5

WHEELS OF JUSTICE

WITH BENJAMIN LACH BEHIND BARS, ACCUSED of the murder of Alice Morgan, the wheels of justice began to turn, with Lubbock County Justice of the Peace Wayne LeCroy scheduling an examining trial for March 25. This first act in what would prove to be a lengthy and complicated legal ordeal featured the sensational testimony of an alibi witness.

Taking center stage was Novis Joan Dominick, a dark-haired, twenty-seven-year-old Tech freshman from Smyer, Texas, who testified that she and Lach drank coffee while visiting at her apartment during the time of the murder on December 4, 1967. She said the two had met up earlier that evening on campus in the Student Union Building.

In describing their relationship, Dominick said she had known Lach "roughly since the middle of September" and characterized him as "more or less a casual friend." The witness said the two became acquainted while Lach tutored a Jewish woman in math, and also indicated that

Lach and she had attended the local synagogue at the same time, although never together.

Defense attorney Bill Gillespie asked Dominick exactly when and where she saw the defendant on the night of the murder.

"Well, it's difficult to recall exactly the time," Dominick replied. "It was around 6:30 p.m. It was in the entrance across from the library [referring to the entrance of the Student Union]," adding they left the Student Union together about ten minutes after meeting.

Gillespie then asked where they went from the Student Union Building.

"Well, we walked to my apartment. He offered to walk me part of the way and that rather surprised me," Dominick said. She stated the apartment was on Third Place, behind the Hi-D-Ho, a popular local drive-in restaurant at College Avenue and Third Place.

Dominick testified that the trip from the Student Union to her apartment normally took about twenty-five minutes to walk, unless it was cold, and then she walked a little faster. At the apartment, she made some coffee and "we sat down and just talked."

Gillespie inquired as to what the two friends talked about.

"Well, about Israel for one thing," Dominick said.

"Can you tell us approximately what time Benjamin Lach left your home that night?" Gillespie asked.

"Well, roughly 9 [o'clock]," Dominick answered. "I didn't pay much attention, but it was around 9."

If Dominick's testimony was accurate, then Lach could not have committed the crime, as Alice Morgan was murdered sometime between 7:30 and 8 p.m. on the night in question.

Under cross-examination by District Attorney Alton Griffin, Dominick admitted that she had been under psychiatric care twice— once in 1964, and once under a ten-day voluntary observation in a St. Louis, Missouri, hospital in 1967. When asked what her psychiatric ailment was in 1964, Dominick said, "I don't know. I had a nervous breakdown or mental breakdown. Specifically, I don't know, you'd have to go through my records."

Despite Dominick's testimony, Judge LeCroy ruled there was enough evidence against Lach to have the case sent to the grand jury, and the accused remained jailed without bond. The legal proceedings continued on April 16, when the 99th District Court Grand Jury returned an indictment of "murder with malice" against Benjamin Lach in the death of Sarah Alice Morgan. Ten days later, Lach was arraigned, and Judge Howard Davison appointed Bill Gillespie and A. W. Salyars as his defense attorneys. Both individuals practiced in Lubbock and were held in high regard in local legal circles.

That fall, in November, a report surfaced that famed criminal defense attorney F. Lee Bailey of Boston might be retained as Lach's counsel. At that point in time, the high-profile Bailey was best known for his work on the Boston Strangler case with suspect Albert DeSalvo, and for his appeal in the case of Dr. Sam Sheppard, a Cleveland physician convicted of murdering his wife.

However, in setting a pretrial hearing for December 5, 1968, Judge Davison and District Attorney Griffin said Bailey would not be representing Lach and the defendant's court-appointed counsel—Gillespie and Salyars—would retain their duties.

Gerald Alch, an associate of Bailey, confirmed this news as well.

"I have advised Mr. Gillespie by letter that we are not going to represent the boy," Alch said. "I have to be vague on the reason why Mr. Bailey was not retained because, frankly, I just don't know." Bailey, however, later told reporters that he had been unable to "come to terms" with Lach's parents.

"His Lubbock attorneys are very capable, very competent," Alch said, "and we feel the boy is in good hands."

The efforts to hire Bailey delayed Lach's sanity hearing, scheduled for late October in the 99th District Court. After Bailey declined involvement, Judge Davison proceeded and set the hearing for December 17; the purpose was to determine whether Lach was sane or insane "at the present time."

According to the *University Daily*, Judge Davison said that if Lach were found insane at the time of the hearing, it would mean he was mentally incompetent to make a rational defense of the charge lodged

Murder suspect Benjamin Lach leaves his sanity hearing accompanied by Lubbock Sheriff's Deputy Jim Howard. (*Lubbock Avalanche-Journal* morgue file collection, the Southwest Collection.)

against him. Therefore, he would not stand trial but instead be admitted to Rusk State Hospital in Rusk, Texas.

"If found sane by that jury, he will be tried for murder," Davison said. "But he can set up a defense on the grounds that he was insane at the time of the alleged commission of the crime."

A jury of ten men and two women was seated on December 17. During the process of questioning the prospective jury members, both

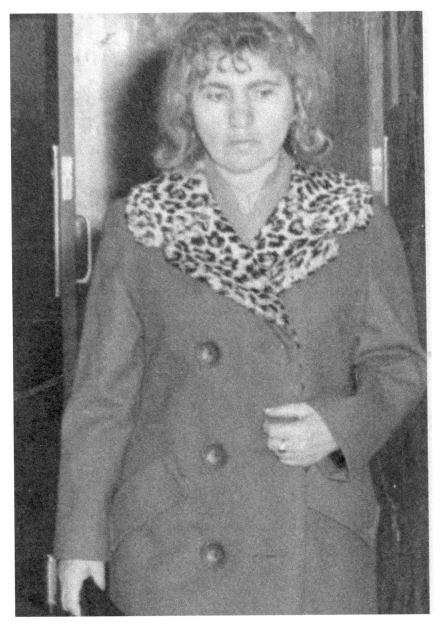

Mrs. Herman Lach walks outside the courtroom after a hearing. (*Lubbock Avalanche-Journal* morgue file collection, the Southwest Collection.)

the prosecution and defense agreed on Lach's lack of mental competence at the present time.

"[Lach] is not capable of communicating properly with his attorneys," DA Griffin said. He added that the case was "unusual" because witnesses for both sides would be testifying for the same result: that Lach was not mentally competent to stand trial.

Defense attorney Gillespie echoed the prosecution's assertion, saying he and co-counsel Salyars "are here to assure you that Benjamin Lach is mentally incompetent at this time."

Lach, dressed in a black suit, sat staring into space or at a side wall, clutching a folded handkerchief. His mother Lucy, a short woman with reddish-brown hair, attended the hearing. On at least two occasions during the proceedings, she put on dark glasses and dabbed her eyes with a flowery handkerchief. Benjamin, sitting quietly, occasionally leaned over to talk to her.

Three local expert witnesses—a clinical psychologist and two psychiatrists—offered testimony.

Dr. Murray Kovnar, the fifty-six-year-old Texas Tech clinical psychologist, was a former New York City policeman who earned a PhD in clinical psychology and a law degree at the University of Denver. He also spent time as chief psychologist at the North Dakota State Hospital and as assistant director in the psychiatric clinic at the Jackson State Prison in Michigan.

A native of Russia, Kovnar came to Lubbock from North Dakota in 1961. The nationally recognized authority in detention and penal rehabilitation was short in stature, but in addition to being a member of the Tech faculty had a limited private practice in Lubbock.

Kovnar related that in late February/early March he administered a series of tests to the suspect, examining him for a total of twenty-one hours. He stated Lach possessed an IQ of about 125, which, Kovnar noted, was "superior, in the top three percent." An IQ of ninety to 110 is considered to be in the "normal" range, the psychologist explained to jurors.

"A personality test," Kovnar said, "definitely showed bizarre responses, perhaps even psychotic." He asked Lach to tell stories about pictures shown to him. "All the stories and protocol suggested some disorganized thinking," Kovnar said.

For example, in a situation where Lach was asked to draw pictures of his family, Kovnar revealed Lach drew a picture of himself that was much taller than the other family members, but with his mother as the dominating factor. Kovnar said the "unconscious portrayal of how a person feels in relation to his family" also indicated "some jealousy toward a brother."

During the testing, Kovnar stated he "had the feeling" that Lach was holding back some information. Sodium pentothal, commonly known as "truth serum," was administered by Dr. John Miller (a Lubbock psychiatrist) to Lach, but, again, "he seemed to have been blocking out key words," Kovnar said. This behavior suggested to Kovnar the suspect's inability to respond without fear of disclosing something.

The witness observed that Lach, even under the influence of the drug and on two polygraph tests, showed "a refusal to respond . . . or inability to respond," particularly when asked about Alice Morgan's keys. "Withholding a response shows a definite reluctance to answer," Kovnar said. "The key was a very dramatic experience; he couldn't talk about it."

Kovnar classified Lach as a paranoid schizophrenic, "one who is overly suspicious, doesn't trust people and who is out of contact with reality."

Dr. Louis Barnes, a local psychiatrist and former director of the South Plains Guidance Center, also testified for the state. The Nashville, Tennessee, native earned his bachelor's degree at Vanderbilt University and his MD at Vanderbilt Medical School. After opening a private practice in Seagraves, Texas, he moved to Topeka, Kansas, to join the renowned Menninger Foundation as a resident in psychiatry in the Veterans Administration Hospital and in the foundation's School of Psychiatry. He started a private practice in Lubbock in 1964.

Barnes told the court he examined Lach on three occasions, for a total of four hours.

"In general, it became apparent that he was living two lives," Barnes said. "The trouble really started when he failed at Boston

University [leaving the school after one semester due to poor grades] ... the aim to succeed was a driving force in him, and he would stop at nothing to succeed."

Barnes said Lach told him about burglarizing a professor's home in Boston because "'he couldn't stand not knowing what his grade was.' It would be three weeks before the grade was posted but he was so over-whelmed by this anxiety that he just had to act like this."

"[Lach] has lived a lie," the psychiatrist said. "He has lied consistently over the past few years." Barnes stated that Lach represented himself as a scholar who knew everything and told people he was making straight A's, but in reality he was failing academically.

Barnes recalled he heard "two different stories" from Lach about events on the day Morgan was murdered. "They were real bizarre, fan-tastic stories, too. Things like that just do not happen except in a novel. I don't think he's trustworthy in anything he says," Barnes said.

Additionally, Barnes indicated that Lach could not tolerate the stresses that "normal people can."

The lone defense witness was Dr. R. K. O'Loughlin, also a psychia-trist and in private practice in Lubbock since 1949. O'Loughlin com-pleted his pre-medical studies at Catholic University in Washington, DC, and earned his MD at Georgetown Medical School. After serving a one-year internship at Georgetown University Hospital, O'Loughlin was a flight surgeon in the armed services during World War II. He opened a general practice in Lubbock in 1945, then returned to school. O'Loughlin attended the Pennsylvania Postgraduate Medical School and served as a resident in psychiatry at the Pennsylvania Hospital.

O'Loughlin related that he interviewed Lach on seven occasions for a total of a little more than nine hours. His diagnostic conclusion showed Lach to be a sociopathic person, whom he described as one demonstrat-ing extreme egotism, repeated and consistent untruthfulness, marked impulsiveness, use and abuse of people to serve one's own gain, and failure to learn from experience.

"I found a preponderance of all five elements—almost a textbook case," O'Loughlin said, adding that Lach was "thoroughly undependable" and should "enter treatment and expect a long-term program."

District Attorney Griffin waived his closing argument, and Gillespie walked around behind Lach and laid a hand on his shoulder.

"We have a human being, just like your child and mine, who is sick," Gillespie told the jury. "He needs help. He needs professional help. Give this boy the same right to hospitalization that you would give to your child."

The jury deliberated only twelve minutes before deciding Lach was insane at the present time and should receive treatment at a state hospital. While his mother Lucy listened to the jury's decision, Benjamin Lach showed no outward expression of emotion.

Judge Davison instructed District Attorney Griffin and defense co-counsels Gillespie and Salyars to collaborate on a written order. When that order was filed, Davison said he would commit Lach to Rusk State Hospital.

"[Lach] was pretty disoriented after he spent some time in jail," Alton Griffin said in an interview several years later. "I think Dr. [Murray] Kovnar was more interested in sending him to Rusk [State Hospital] to start with."

"I give a lot of credit to Dr. Kovnar [for understanding Lach]," Blair Cherry said, reflecting on the case. He continued:

> Murray Kovnar was Jewish and an immigrant [like Lach]. He came as a child about the time of the "Fiddler on the Roof" immigration of Jews from Russia. . . . He was a lawyer and a PhD in psychology. Because of this, he seemed a perfect choice to help us unravel what Benjamin Lach was all about.
>
> [Kovnar] agreed to give Lach a series of psychological tests and provide us with his conclusions. Lach agreed to this . . . throughout, he was always very cooperative and agreeable. Murray ran the series of tests. . . . I am sure one of them was the Minnesota Multiphasic

Personality Inventory, but I cannot remember the others. The next Sunday morning I got a call from Murray. The first thing he asked for was police protection. He was genuinely frightened by what he had figured out about Lach. I calmed him down, and he told me what his results were. Lach was indeed a sociopathic personality. He had a compulsion about grades because of his mother's great ambitions for him.

Murray also made reference to the experiences Lach had as a young child in Israel, where he apparently had to assist his father in the koshering process several times. He thought that that was what Lach had done to Mrs. Morgan . . . that he had "koshered" her. That would account for the very large amount of blood at the scene. . . . Kovnar's work assisted us in determining how to trap Lach, and how to pressure him.

According to Jewish dietary guidelines, meat or poultry is soaked in clean water for thirty minutes, then removed to drip dry. After a few minutes of dripping, the meat is salted and left to hang for sixty minutes to further draw out any remaining blood.

Cherry also emphasized the importance of properly questioning the suspect.

Once [during the investigation] we had done the background checks on Lach, he was talked to, I think, by Alton, but I'm not sure. Various discrepancies were noted in his story, and he was asked to take a lie detector test. He agreed and met me at the DPS [Department of Public Safety] office, where [examiner] Tom Barnes did the test. I watched the test through a one-way glass. During the test, which was gone through five times, the chart consistently showed no reaction to the questions, even though he lied about a number of things that we knew he was lying about. The only reaction on the entire test was the galvanometer on the last question about the master key that was taken at the time of the murder. We told him that he had failed the test, and he left. . . . Tom and I discussed the results after Lach had gone and came to the conclusion that we were dealing with a socio-pathic personality that had no scruples about lying. Tom was the one who recommended that we consult with Dr. Kovnar to get a better understanding of Lach.

SIDEBAR: F. LEE BAILEY AND O. J. SIMPSON

Many years after the Lach case, F. Lee Bailey returned to the national spotlight by joining the legal "dream team" that successfully defended former pro football star O. J. Simpson. The dream team consisted of Bailey, Robert Shapiro, Johnnie Cochran, and others. Simpson was acquitted in the June 12, 1994, murders of his ex-wife and her friend. Many observers dubbed the trial, held in Los Angeles and tele-vised nationally, as the "trial of the century." In Simpson's heyday in the 1970s as an athlete and celebrity, he did a series of TV commer-cials for Hertz Rent-a-Car, the company Benjamin Lach worked for in Lubbock.

SIDEBAR: THE BAYLOR COED MURDER

On May 27, 1968, Jackie W. Grider was sentenced to die in the elec-tric chair for the December 1967 murder of Baylor coed Jill Brown of Crawford, Texas. During the trial, it was revealed that Grider confessed to the murder and led officers to the murder weapon (hunting knife) and the victim's car keys.

Grider said that on the day of the murder, he went to a Waco shop-ping center, told Brown he couldn't get his pickup to start, and asked for a ride to a service station. He then forced her to drive to a secluded area, pushed her into the back seat and raped her. After she threatened to go to the police, Grider struck Brown on the head with the butt of his hunting knife, stabbed her, and dumped the body.

Psychiatrists testified that Grider had "schizoid to sociopathic ten-dencies." Other testimony stated that Grider had undergone psychiatric treatment on three occasions, beginning when he was eleven years old.

Grider eventually received a new trial, but the second trial, held in March 1972, yielded the same sentence: death in the electric chair. He died in prison (Eastham Unit) on July 19, 1995, at age fifty-two.

CHAPTER 6

RUSK STATE
HOSPITAL

RUSK STATE HOSPITAL IS NESTLED ON A HILLSIDE in the deep, lush Piney Woods of East Texas in small-town Rusk (population 5,000), approximately 128 miles southeast of Dallas, about the same distance northeast of Houston, and a fifty-minute drive south of Tyler, Texas.

It might as well be worlds away from the flat, dusty south plains of West Texas. One 1970 newspaper article described Rusk as "old, with well-kept lawns, pine trees, shrubbery, and a small lake." The hospital looked as if it came straight out of a 1950s Hollywood movie that depicted mental institutions with white column buildings, as stern attendants in white uniforms walked with patients on quiet, serene grounds.

The Rusk State Hospital for the Mentally Ill opened in 1919 with the conversion of the Rusk Penitentiary building into a hospital for the care of the "Negro insane." Prior to that, construction on the original three-story penitentiary was completed in 1878, and prisoners assisted in building a railroad from Rusk to Palestine, as well as an iron ore smelting furnace adjacent to the administration building.

The prison closed in 1917, and the Texas Legislature appropriated funds for its conversion into a mental hospital. During its first year of operation, some of the old penitentiary buildings were renovated, reconstructed, and converted into wards and hospital buildings, with 600 patients admitted.

By 1946, the Rusk State Hospital housed 2,308 patients but held a capacity of 2,426. The average daily census of patients at the hospital dropped to 1,942 in 1964. By 1967, the number fell to 1,700 patients, and a maximum-security unit for the criminally insane housed 320 patients.

Early in its history, the institution included a general hospital for the care of the acutely sick, an infirmary for aged and decrepit cases, a tubercular hospital for the care of white men and women, and a tubercular hospital for Black men and women. A chapel, occupational therapy shop, recreational hall, and picnic area for visitors were added later. Rusk operated its own garden, farms, hog ranch, and poultry farm, which supplied much of its needs.

Prison-like fences surrounded the hospital, and it wasn't until 1968, when Dr. Arch Connolly became superintendent, that flowers began replacing fences and a blanket of bright colors covered the cold gray dullness of the hospital. Much of the barbed wire and grates were knocked down, and painters replaced the gray color scheme with yellows, greens, and reds.

But behind the hospital, perched on what is known as hospital hill, stood the maximum-security unit, which opened in 1953. A pair of fifteen-foot electric fences, topped by barbed wire, with guard towers in two corners, surrounded the unit. Murderers, rapists, psychopaths, and other violent offenders inhabited the triangular-shaped maximum-security complex. At one time, it was known by the rather awkward and direct name of "Rusk State Hospital for the Criminally Insane."

As one might imagine, it was not an ideal place in which to live. Most patients received some form of medication (anti-psychotic drugs) and were awakened at six o'clock in the morning in their barrack-like build-ings to do daily clean-up duty or farm work. Their regimented days were much like those in a penitentiary and even included occasional random acts of violence in the recreational hall.

The second-floor cells were reserved for patients who exhibited dan-gerous behavior, and their world consisted of a small room, a steel door, concrete walls, and barred windows. But those patients who showed a willingness to cooperate had access to a special privilege ward, with perks such as televisions, phonographs, pool tables, and, most important, windows without bars.

Benjamin Lach entered Rusk on December 18, 1968, and by early 1970 reports surfaced that he was progressing well and might soon return to Lubbock. On February 12, 1970, J. Blair Cherry, by then Lubbock County district attorney, and defense attorney Bill Gillespie traveled to Rusk to confer with hospital officials about Lach's status.

"Just what action will be taken will depend on a staff meeting in a few days," said Dr. J. A. Hunter, a physician in charge of the maximum-security unit at Rusk. "At the meeting," he told the *A-J,* "we will decide whether we will recommend to the superintendent that he be certified back to Lubbock. Lach has been given routine periodic review . . . and it looks pretty good. Apparently he has gotten the impres-sion he's improving and imminently will be certified back . . . he's already written his folks. At the present time he has responded very well and has done fine. Right now it's just too early to speculate on just what will be done."

Hunter also told the newspaper that Lach had apparently been impressed by "the extra attention he's getting lately and has assumed that he more or less has done well."

By March, a decision had been reached, and on March 6, 1970, Benjamin Lach returned to the Lubbock County Jail, pending another sanity hearing.

He arrived in Lubbock wearing a short-sleeved shirt and denim jeans. Lach's personal belongings were placed in a large wooden box

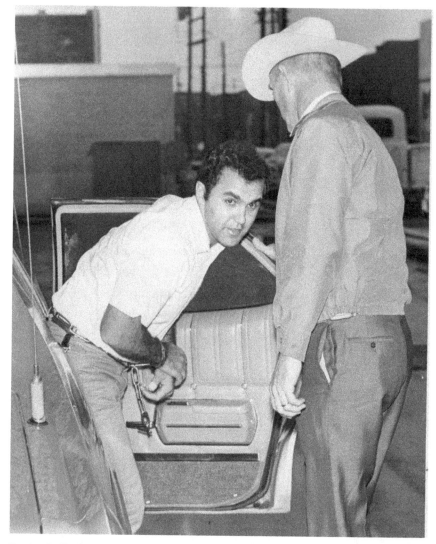

Benjamin Lach returns to Lubbock for a sanity hearing in 1970 after a stay in Rusk State Hospital. (*Lubbock Avalanche-Journal* morgue file collection, the Southwest Collection.)

that he had built at Rusk, and he told one jailer that he had gained "a little weight" while at the hospital.

Things began to move swiftly as 99th District Court Judge Howard Davison held a daylong hearing on April 8 to determine if Lach was mentally competent to stand trial for the murder of Alice Morgan. The twelve-man jury heard two witnesses—Dr. Hunter and Dr. Kovnar—disagree as to whether Lach was legally sane or insane.

Dr. Hunter, the Rusk physician and the state's lone witness, testified that Lach was mentally competent to stand trial. He diagnosed Lach's condition as an "antisocial personality" and said Lach exhibited no irrational behavior. "As far as we were concerned," Hunter said, "he was at all time in contact with reality."

In response to a question from District Attorney Cherry, Hunter said, "No, in my opinion, [Lach] does not require further treatment. We found nothing, actually, to treat while he was there."

According to Hunter, Lach's antisocial personality was characterized by extreme egotism, marked impulsiveness, failure to learn from experience, using people for his own gain, and repeated and consistent untruthfulness. The physician observed, however, that these characteristics were not as prominent in Lach as they might be in other patients.

Hunter stated that Lach's treatment at Rusk consisted of remotivation and resocialization, which he described as "training or encouraging the patient to get along at peace with his fellow man." He said Lach volunteered to teach classes for the mentally disabled and the illiterate patients at the state hospital and participated in small theater and musical groups.

Taking the opposite viewpoint was Dr. Kovnar, the Texas Tech clinical psychologist who first examined Lach prior to his arrest in 1968 and then again after his return from the state hospital. The defense witness told the jury that in 1968 he had initially diagnosed Lach as a "paranoid schizophrenic and definitely in need of treatment."

"What change, if any, has occurred since that time?" Gillespie asked.

"I found the results basically to be the same," Kovnar said. "It was a little more difficult this time because he was a little more experienced. He wasn't as open as he was . . . more guarded. But I would still call him a paranoid schizophrenic."

"At this time," Gillespie continued, "would you say that Ben is competent to aid in a defense against the charge?"

"Well, in all fairness to Ben, he may be rational at times, but it is pretty hard to tell if he will be the same every day," Kovnar said.

During closing arguments, defense attorneys Gillespie and Salyars pointedly criticized Hunter and the state hospital system.

"This boy [Lach] was entitled to treatment," Salyars said. "The court here sent him to Rusk to get treatment. But he didn't get any. They did it the lazy way. They labeled him antisocial and put him to work teaching in their school. Are we going to let our state institutions handle their responsibility that way?"

Gillespie said, "Ben was there [at Rusk] for fifteen months and interviewed four times by a general practitioner [Dr. Hunter]." He noted that Hunter had stated that there were nine doctors on the staff at Rusk State Hospital for more than 1,700 patients.

Salyars suggested that his client might be better served by transferring to another hospital: "If you take an auto to one place and they don't repair it, you don't have to take it back to the same place."

Cherry countered by telling the jury Hunter's experience qualified him for membership in the American Psychiatric Association. He also asked the jury to consider the testimony of a doctor who, with staff psychologists, had observed Lach for nearly fifteen months, while the defense's expert witness (Kovnar) had tested the defendant for only two hours.

Hunter graduated from Baylor University and the University of Texas Medical School in Galveston. Prior to joining the staff at Rusk, he spent twenty-plus years with the United States Public Health Service (USPHS). Hunter once served on a Coast Guard ship, part of a Navy squadron that invaded Guam. He also traveled to Antarctica with Adm. Richard Byrd. His professional experience included stints at USPHS hospitals in Massachusetts, Maryland, Michigan, Missouri, Alaska, and New Jersey.

Lach sat quietly throughout the hearing, chatting with his mother. Neither exhibited any outward emotion when the jury, after deliberating for an hour and fifty-five minutes, delivered its decision: Benjamin Lach was mentally competent to stand trial for the December 4, 1967, murder of Sarah Alice Morgan.

Benjamin Lach is escorted out of the 99th District courtroom during a break in his sanity hearing. (*Lubbock Avalanche-Journal* morgue file collection, the Southwest Collection.)

The state immediately announced it would seek the death penalty.

In an ironic twist of fate, Lubbock psychiatrist Dr. Louis Barnes, who testified in Lach's original sanity hearing, was deceased by the time of the second hearing. The forty-three-year-old physician was stabbed to death in the bedroom of his Lubbock home on September 24, 1969. And just after Lach returned to Lubbock from Rusk, Madeline Simmonds Barnes, the psychiatrist's thirty-eight-year-old wife, was transported to Rusk. Charged with her husband's murder, Madeline Barnes was ruled mentally incompetent to stand trial.

Dr. Murray Kovnar's family also experienced violent crime. About eighteen months after the second sanity hearing, Kovnar died of a heart attack in Lubbock on October 17, 1971, at age fifty-nine. Five years later, his twenty-nine-year-old daughter was abducted while working at a 7–Eleven convenience store in El Paso. Mrs. Sima Kovnar Warren, wife and mother of two young sons, was robbed, beaten, raped, and dumped in the Rio Grande, where she drowned. The case, never officially solved, had notorious serial killers Henry Lee Lucas and Ottis Toole claiming responsibility for the horrific crime.

SIDEBAR: ROKY AT RUSK

Musician Roger "Roky" Erickson and Lach were in Rusk together for some five months (October 1969 to March 1970). Erickson played in one of America's first psychedelic rock bands, the 13th Floor Elevators, with their most famous song being "You're Gonna Miss Me," a 1966 hit.

Erickson arrived at Rusk after being declared "insane" in connection with his arrest for possession of marijuana. His attorney had advised him to plead insanity in order to avoid prison time. (He originally took up residence in the Austin State Hospital but escaped the minimum-security facility.)

A teenager named James Wolcott also resided in Rusk during this time (1968–1974). On August 14, 1967, the fifteen-year-old returned to his Georgetown, Texas, home after attending a rock concert in Austin. After sniffing model airplane glue, Wolcott grabbed a .22 rifle and proceeded to shoot to death his father, mother, and sister.

During Erickson's confinement, he formed a rock band (The Missing Links), which included young Wolcott on guitar, a bass guitarist, a drummer, and a deaf tambourine player. All, with the exception of Erickson, were accused murderers.

Erickson received various medications during a torturous three years at Rusk, finally gaining his release in late 1972. Afterward, he experienced a number of "ups" and "downs," and sporadically continued his musical career. He died in 2019 at age seventy-one.

SIDEBAR: LUBBOCK'S MOST INFAMOUS CRIMINAL, JOHN HINCKLEY JR.

John Hinckley Jr. is probably the most "infamous" criminal with ties to Lubbock and Texas Tech.

On March 30, 1981, Hinckley shot and wounded President Ronald Reagan and three others outside the Hilton Hotel in Washington, DC.

Hinckley, a member of an affluent Dallas family, attended Texas Tech off and on for several years (1974–1980), majoring first in business and then in English. He never graduated, however. On discovering Hinckley's West Texas connections, the national media arrived in Lubbock to paint a not-so-flattering portrait of Texas Tech:

"Academically modest," is how *Newsweek* magazine described Tech.

"Prosaic state-run university on the dusty flatlands of the Texas Panhandle," offered the *Wall Street Journal*.

And there was this gem from the *Washington Post*: "A penchant for guns hardly strikes anyone as ominous in free-wheeling Lubbock, where some university students carry guns to class."

One month after Hinckley wounded the president, the following correction appeared in the *Post*: "An article in the April 5 edition of the *Washington Post* presented an inaccurate depiction of Texas Tech University and the city in which the university is located, Lubbock. Texas Tech students do not carry guns to class, as the article stated, and the city itself is a quiet town with orderly and law-abiding citizens. There is no 'pistol-packing' tradition in Lubbock, as the article incorrectly implied."

In a controversial court case, Hinckley was found not guilty by reason of insanity and confined to St. Elizabeth's Hospital in Washington, DC. In 2021, he was given his unconditional release from the hospital, effective in 2022.

Hinckley, while in Lubbock in the late 1970s, lived in various apartments, including the Honeycomb Apartments in 1980, which still stand today (known as The Square at South Overton)—just a short walk from Main Street, where Benjamin Lach resided in 1967–1968.

CHAPTER 7

ON TRIAL

AFTER TWO SANITY HEARINGS AND A FIFTEEN- month confinement in Rusk State Hospital, Benjamin Lach would finally stand trial for the gruesome murder of Texas Tech custodian Sarah Alice Morgan.

On June 8, 1970, Lubbock County 99th District Court Judge Howard C. Davison granted an uncontested defense motion for a change of venue. Due to the widespread publicity of the case throughout the Lubbock area, the trial moved east to the Criminal District Court No. 1 in Fort Worth, Texas, with Judge Byron Matthews presiding.

Judge Matthews scheduled a pretrial hearing for July 16, but "missing defense witnesses" caused a delay until fall. The judge then set the trial date for September 21 and appointed a local public defender, Dawson "Doss" Davis, to assist the defense team.

Still more delays followed, and on September 21, Judge Matthews granted a continuance to the defense to allow more time to line up witnesses.

The no-nonsense, fifty-eight-year-old Matthews was well respected by those in the legal profession and was labeled with such nicknames as "Little Caesar," "Byron the Baron," and "Paddle Man." Judge Matthews, described by one lawyer as "tough as a boot," had a particular disdain for longhaired defendants, often ordering the offenders to get a haircut if they expected leniency.

At the young age of twenty-two, the Baylor Law School graduate started his career as a prosecutor in 1934. Prior to his election to the judgeship in 1962, Matthews was reputed to be one of the state's outstanding criminal defense lawyers, representing some of Tarrant County's most notorious gangsters, gamblers, and hoodlums.

Fort Worth public defender Davis joined court-appointed Lubbock attorneys Bill Gillespie and A. W. "Shorty" Salyars to complete the defense team. F. Lee Bailey notwithstanding, the courtroom would not be lacking in skilled lawyering—on either side of the table.

In addition to being seasoned criminal trial lawyers with forty-five years of experience between them, Gillespie and Salyars both had extensive tenure as prosecutors on their resumes. William Joe "Bill" Gillespie had served as Lubbock County attorney with none other than Alton Griffin as his assistant county attorney in the late 1950s. Gillespie entered private practice on July 1, 1960, with fifteen years of legal work to his credit.

Salyars also brought experience as a prosecutor, serving as Dallam County (far northwest Texas) attorney for five years before opening a private practice in Lubbock in 1947. The following year, he was appointed Lubbock County assistant district attorney and, in 1950, filed to run for the office of DA. Salyars later changed his mind and on April 1, 1950, resigned to reenter private practice.

The University of Texas Law School graduate's thirty-year career in the courtroom offered a collection of colorful stories. Nicknamed "Shorty" because of his diminutive height, the fifty-four-year-old was regarded by his peers as not only intelligent but very resourceful. During final arguments in one criminal case, Salyars pulled his handkerchief out to wipe the tears away as he pleaded for leniency for his client. The argument proved effective, and the client did indeed receive probation. It was later "discovered" that Salyars generated the

Lubbock County Criminal District Attorney Blair Cherry (pictured) and Special Prosecutor Alton Griffin presented the state's case in the trial of Benjamin Lach. Cherry later served as a district judge for many years. (*Lubbock Avalanche-Journal* morgue file collection, the Southwest Collection.)

"tears" by hiding snuff in his handkerchief and then rubbing his eyes with the cloth.

The prosecution team of Lubbock County District Attorney J. Blair Cherry Jr. and Special Prosecutor Alton Griffin proved to be equally formidable.

The youthful Cherry, age thirty-one, possessed a bright and

promising future in the field of law. He was the son of former University of Texas football coach-turned-oilman J. Blair Cherry. A multisport athlete at Lubbock Monterey High School, Cherry Jr. excelled in track. After graduating from UT Law School in 1964, he began his career in private practice in Midland, Texas. In addition to his law practice, Cherry taught seventh and eighth grade social studies and coached football and track in the West Texas town during the 1965–1966 school year.

Cherry was named assistant district attorney in Lubbock under Griffin in 1966 and a year later was appointed first assistant. He replaced Griffin as district attorney on January 1, 1969. In contrast to Salyars, Cherry stood six foot one, weighed 208 pounds, and wore dark-framed eyeglasses. Although born in Austin, he was raised in Lubbock.

Those in the know related how Cherry rarely raised his voice in the courtroom.

"I believe a low-key presentation would be a pretty good description," one judge said of Cherry. "As I've observed him, he's been pretty effective with it. He has good rapport with juries and leaves a feeling of respect for his sincerity."

Out of the courtroom, Cherry enjoyed such pastimes as gardening (both vegetable and flower), fishing, and handball.

Griffin also earned his law degree at the University of Texas, in 1956, and went to work as Lubbock assistant county attorney, first under legendary Lubbock County DA Travis Shelton, and then under Gillespie for three years. Running unopposed, Griffin was elected county attorney in 1960, and he took the reins as Lubbock County district attorney in 1962 and served in that capacity through 1968.

Griffin, forty-three, was in private practice when appointed as special prosecutor by Cherry. The Crowell, Texas, native actively participated in civic affairs, most notably with the Lubbock Lions Club. Years later, when asked about the state's team, Cherry said: "Alton was the DA when

Alton Griffin was special prosecutor in the trial
of Benjamin Lach. Griffin was Lubbock district
attorney at the time of the Morgan murder.
He served as a prosecutor from 1956 to 1978,
except for three years when he was in private
practice. (Author collection.)

the offense occurred and was instrumental in the investigation of the
case. . . . I had money [$5,000] in the budget, and Alton wanted to do
it, so I thought it would be in everyone's interest to bring him aboard."

"All I had to do was talk—try the case," Griffin recalled. "Blair did
all the legwork and did it well."

Griffin spoke highly of defense attorneys Salyars and Gillespie.
"Salyars was a spellbinder, an outstanding trial lawyer who never left
anything unturned."

The prosecution scored a pair of major victories during the pretrial hearing. First, Judge Matthews overruled a defense motion which, if granted, would have prohibited the state from seeking the death penalty. The judge also partially granted a motion that would have suppressed media coverage of the pretrial hearing. He ordered newspaper and television cameramen not to photograph the defendant, any witnesses, or attorneys in the case unless the respective person granted permission. Further, Judge Matthews requested the Fort Worth media not mention Lach's alleged confession in advance news accounts of the trial, as to do so could jeopardize the selection of an impartial jury.

As the pretrial began, Tom Barnes, a Department of Public Safety polygraph examiner, testified that Lach showed a "reaction each time he was asked about the killing" of Alice Morgan during a second series of tests. Barnes said he examined the defendant on February 8, 1968, and again on February 12, 1968. He said the first polygraph exam was "inconclusive," but that during the second test, Lach showed a reaction when asked about the murder.

Still another key victory for the prosecution came when Judge Matthews admitted into evidence a statement made by Lach concerning his involvement in the murder. The defense had filed a motion to suppress the statement on the grounds that if Lach had made such a statement, it was obtained "only after duress and repeated harassment by investigators."

The two individuals who took the statement from the defendant emphatically contradicted the claim made by the prosecution. Capt. Carrol G. Bartley of the Lubbock Police Department and Alton Griffin (district attorney at the time the statement was made) both testified that Lach had made the statement voluntarily and only after being advised of his rights.

The defense did, however, convince the judge to allow another audiotape recording to be entered into evidence. This tape had been sent anonymously to the Tech Security-Police Office, only to have the authorities discount the taped confession as a hoax.

The voice on the tape said:

> I thought I ought to talk to somebody and tell somebody what I did.
> I just did it, that's all. I go over and sit in the cafeteria and nobody
> even talks to me. They sit there and look at me like I am some kind
> of freak. I know I killed the old lady, but I didn't mean to do it. The
> old lady came in there and I just cut her. I'm crazy, I know that, but
> I'm not crazy enough to walk into a cop house and say I did it. I need
> help, I know that. If you think she was bleeding, you should have seen
> me. The old lady stuck me in the arm. And if you guys are worth your
> salt you will know where to find me.

Jury selection began on October 26, and eleven men and one woman
were seated, with Lach pleading not guilty to the charges of murder
with malice.

A small courtroom in the Tarrant County Criminal Courts Building
served as the backdrop for the drama about to unfold.

On Monday, November 2, 1970, almost three years after the murder
of Sarah Alice Morgan, testimony began in the trial of her accused killer.
Prosecutors subpoenaed fifty-six witnesses, while defense attorneys summoned fifteen potential witnesses.

The three-week trial would have its share of drama but, alas, no Perry
Mason magic revelation at its conclusion.

Texas Tech custodian Macie Mathis took the stand on day one and
testified that she discovered the body of her coworker, Sarah Alice
Morgan, face up in a pool of blood in Room 304-J of the Tech Science
Building on December 4, 1967. Mathis explained that she and other custodians noticed Morgan's failure to appear for their usual supper break
at 8 p.m. Mathis then went to the third floor in search of her colleague,
where she knew Alice Morgan had been cleaning. Arriving there, she
noticed Morgan's trash cart outside the lab (304-J). After discovering the
body, she summoned her supervisor, John C. Hightower, who was also
looking for the missing custodian. Immediately, Hightower instructed

Mathis to call the police, but the understandably shaken custodian dialed the college telephone operator by mistake.

Mathis, employed as a Tech custodian since 1962, further testified that Morgan was always careful with her building keys, keeping them pinned to the inside of her dress pocket. She said the slain woman's pocket had been torn off her dress, lying near her body—Morgan's keys were gone, she stated.

Among other witnesses testifying for the state on the first day were Lubbock Police Capt. James Fergerson, Lubbock Police Sgt. Bob Tedder, former Tech student Marilyn Ehrlich, and Tech biology professor Dr. Francis Rose.

Fergerson provided a graphic description of the crime scene, including the revelation that Morgan's head was nearly severed. The prosecution then entered into evidence two murder weapons—a scalpel and a piece of broken bone saw—that Fergerson testified he found near the body. As jurors viewed the weapons, Lach leaned forward with his chin resting in his cupped hands. Later, the defendant ran his fingers nervously through his curly black hair.

Tedder offered additional testimony pertaining to the crime scene, stating that he saw blood on a doorjamb in the lab where Morgan's body was found, perhaps indicating she had struggled with her assailant before she was slain.

Ehrlich, described in one newspaper account as an "attractive housewife," told the court she observed the defendant standing in the third-floor hallway of the Science Building about an hour before Morgan's body was discovered. She said that she, her husband, and their infant daughter arrived at the Science Building about 6:30 that night, as her husband Tracy was conducting research in his third-floor office.

Ehrlich stated that as she and her daughter were walking down the hallway, she noticed a man standing at the other end. "He jumped a little when he heard our footsteps," Ehrlich said. "He turned around and looked at me and then ran down the stairs."

Ehrlich said that at approximately 6:45 p.m., she and her daughter stopped to talk to Morgan as the custodian paused from her duties. Later, as the Ehrlich family left the building, Lach walked out ahead of them, she said.

Defense attorney Gillespie asked Ehrlich if she knew Lach personally; she indicated that she did not but was positive that he was the man she saw there that night. Ehrlich said she first identified Lach to *A-J* reporter Dave Knapp about a month after the murder. Initially, Knapp showed her a Tech ID card with Lach's photograph, but she was unable to identify him from that picture. Knapp then offered her photos of Lach and other men, and Ehrlich identified Lach as the man she saw in the hallway of the Science Building.

Another witness, Dr. Herschel Garner, by then assistant professor of biology at Tarleton State College in Stephenville, Texas, told the court that on the night of December 4, 1967, he saw Lach walk up the stairs to the third floor of the Science Building at about seven o'clock. At the time of the murder, Garner was a Tech student.

Also offering key testimony was the professor in whose lab Morgan's lifeless body was found. Biology professor Francis Rose stated that he occupied the third-floor laboratory (304-J) and identified the broken bone saw as part of his lab equipment. Rose said he had seen Lach twice on the night of the murder, the first time being in the north attic on the third floor at approximately 6:30 p.m. as Rose walked to his lab. When Rose exited the lab to go to the second floor, he saw Lach again, standing in the doorway of Room 204 (a classroom). "I did not know his name, but I knew him by sight," the professor said.

Rose also said that he (Rose) walked out of the biology class he was teaching that night. The professor said he was away from his second-floor classroom "eight or eighteen seconds."

During cross-examination, Gillespie asked Rose if it would surprise him "if one of your students testified that you were gone longer than that?" Gillespie also asked if it would surprise Rose if one of his students claimed the professor changed shirts that night, apparently referring to Captain Fergerson's testimony that a bloody shirt, size 15 1/2-34, was found in a campus trash can.

To both questions, Rose answered that it would not surprise him. Still under cross-examination, Rose said that he agreed to take a polygraph examination after the slaying.

"I was told by police that I flunked it," Rose testified. He added that he was told that several other persons had flunked similar lie detector tests given by Lubbock police during the investigation.

Rose also said that he was with police on the morning after the murder, when an identification card and coin purse belonging to Morgan were discovered in his lab. "Isn't it strange that they were not found that [previous] night?" Gillespie asked the witness. "It certainly is strange," Rose answered, noting that the two items were found underneath a counter in the room just a few feet from where Morgan's body lay.

Following the murder and continuing throughout the investigation, Rose maintained a detailed written log chronicling the events. He also assisted police in creating a composite sketch of an individual seen on the third floor of the Science Building on the night of the murder. Colleagues and others oftentimes offered information to Rose about the case, which he, in turn, passed along to authorities—following Lach's arrest, Rose gave copies of his "diary" to investigators and the *A-J*.

Throughout the daylong testimony, Benjamin Lach sat at the defense table, dressed conservatively in a dark suit, white shirt, and dark tie. His mother, Lucy Lach, having traveled to Lubbock from her Massachusetts home, listened to the testimony and, during recess, walked to the front of the courtroom where her son sat and spoke softly to him.

Lubbock Police Sgt. F. C. "Butch" Hargrave took the stand the next day to describe the stakeout of Room 324 of the Tech Science Building on March 12–13, 1968. Hargrave told the court that he and Lt. Frank Wiley waited throughout the night for a person believed to have been entering the office illegally to obtain copies of tests. Hargrave testified that at about 7:25 a.m. on March 13, the Lubbock policemen heard footsteps in the hallway.

"A key was put in the lock and the door opened a couple of inches—then it hesitated," Hargrave said. "After a few seconds, the door opened and Lach walked in." As Lach entered the office of Dr. Kent Rylander, Hargrave said, Wiley called Lach by name—at that point, Lach and Hargrave were less than three feet apart.

"He dropped his books and ran out and down the stairs," Hargrave said.

And in his haste to flee, Lach left a master key in the lock of the door.

Defense attorney Gillespie pointedly asked Hargrave why he wasn't able to capture Lach.

"Isn't it a fact that you and Wiley were asleep when he entered the room?" Gillespie asked.

"No," replied Hargrave. "I was standing right by the door."

In an attempt to show that it was not possible to identify the master key Lach used to open Room 324 as being the same key stolen from the murdered woman, Gillespie cross-examined two Tech maintenance/building directors.

Ray Downing, director of building maintenance and utilities, and Charles Libby, director of building operations, both testified that records of keys issued to custodians are maintained, but that keys are not serially numbered for identification.

"Isn't it a fact that any good locksmith could duplicate the keys?" Gillespie asked.

Downing agreed that it might be possible but said, "We have a great deal of confidence in our employees."

Dr. John Ray Jr., a Lubbock pathologist, also testified for the prosecution. According to Ray, Morgan died from a loss of blood, adding that the victim was almost decapitated and her voice box and esophagus had been severed. He noted that Morgan also sustained several bruises to her chest, arms, and hands, as well as a severe bruise above her right ear.

The afternoon session began with former Tech student Lucy Cogdell relating that she was studying in the Tech Library on the night of December 4, 1967. Between 8:30 p.m. and 9:00 p.m., she observed a man she identified as Lach enter the basement of the library and sit near her. Cogdell said Lach wore a dark blue shirt, the same clothes several other witnesses testified seeing him wearing earlier that night in the Science Building.

Lach drew her attention, Cogdell said, because of his short, stocky build, his "swarthy coloring and his curly black hair," and the fact that he kept looking at his hands. She said Lach stared at his hands intermittently for about thirty minutes, that he broke off several of his fingernails, and then left the library.

One of Lach's professors, Dr. Kent Rylander, assistant professor of biology, testified that in March 1968 he reported to campus police that his office (324) in the Science Building had been entered after hours and a filing cabinet containing quizzes and grade records was tampered with. In fall 1967, at the time of the Morgan slaying, Lach was in Rylander's Comparative Vertebrate Anatomy class. And at the time (spring 1968) Rylander's office had been illegally entered, Lach was enrolled in Rylander's embryology class.

The bearded professor recalled that early in the fall semester, Lach "was not doing well . . . he made very erratic grades, ranging from as low as 4 [out of 100] to the 60s and 70s." However, after the murder, Rylander said, Lach's grades improved.

Shortly before the trial, Rylander had returned to the United States after being out of the country on sabbatical.

Also called to testify was Lubbock patrolman Emmett Caddell, who observed Lach driving a stolen car and then pursued him until his ultimate capture in Resthaven Cemetery. After fleeing the Science Building, Lach had reportedly stolen the Pontiac from Lubbock resident Judy Beavers.

Unaware the driver of the stolen vehicle was being sought for questioning in a murder, Caddell stopped the driver shortly after he left a gas station. As the officer approached the parked car, Lach told him to "stand back or he would hurt me." Caddell said he stepped aside as Lach suddenly accelerated. A number of police officers then joined the erratic, high-speed chase that ultimately crashed into the cemetery.

On cross-examination, Caddell admitted he kicked Lach as the suspect was being held by four other police officers during his apprehension at Resthaven.

"He was kicked. I did it, which I am sorry to say," Caddell said. "My foot contact was more or less a gesture . . . as far as I know there was no need to kick him." He said he kicked Lach because "I asked him why he drove bad and he said he did not drive bad. I said, 'oh, go on,' and kicked him sideways across the rump." Caddell was later reprimanded by the police department for this action.

After the testimony of Rylander and Caddell, the state entered into evidence the statement given by Lach to authorities on March 13, 1968, the day he was arrested and a little more than three months after the murder. In the statement, Lach admitted going to the Science Building about an hour before Morgan's body was discovered. Furthermore, Lach said he went into several rooms in the building before he first spotted Morgan:

> I was looking around Dr. Rylander's office and she saw me.
>
> I just went into the last room, it had no windows and it was a laboratory . . . where Mrs. Morgan was found . . . and I just went in there in the corner and I was hoping I would wait long enough where there would be no one there.
>
> I didn't see anyone come in the hall section there, then suddenly I heard a noise. Mrs. Morgan came with that basket on wheels and I was standing in the corner and she emptied the trash out.
>
> When she walked out, I came from behind her. I think I strangled her and she fell to the floor. She was still breathing. Afterwards, I decided to cut her up.
>
> I had on my mind that it was either she tells everybody that I was snooping around or I would just quiet her down by killing her and this was only when it came to mind at the time. When she hit the floor she was barely breathing.

In the rambling statement, read by special prosecutor Alton Griffin, Lach said he then looked around and saw a scalpel:

It was on one of the benches there, and so I used the scalpel and I guess I was cutting her throat. I don't remember doing it and I know later that there was a puddle of blood and I remember stepping in it once.

Lach further said in the three-page statement, which was transcribed from a tape recording, that he grabbed the custodian's keys after Morgan appeared to be dead:

I ripped them [the keys] off her dress or skirt, or whatever she had on. Then I turned the lights off when I left. There was blood on the switch. I locked the door from the inside. When I walked out I had blood on my hands but I didn't have any blood anywhere else except the bottom of my feet.

In the statement, Lach said he tried to wipe the blood off his hands and the door knob. After taking the master keys to the offices and classrooms, Lach said he went to Rylander's office "to see if it was open but it was closed and I didn't bother anything." He then walked down the stairs and out of the Science Building and rode his bicycle to the Student Union Building:

The first thing I did was go to the bathroom and wash my hands. Then I went by the color TV and saw the shows were changing, which was 8 p.m. I didn't stay too long because I had my notebook with me and I wanted to look at my notes. So I went to the library and stayed there until about 11 p.m. and then went home.

Lach also admitted in the statement that the key he used to get into Rylander's office on March 13, 1968, "was one of the keys that I took from Mrs. Morgan." (Years later, in an interview, Griffin said investigators never found Morgan's other keys and that Lach had told them that he threw them down a sewer drain.)

The state then rested its case, and defense attorneys Bill Gillespie and A. W. Salyars immediately asked Judge Matthews to order a directed

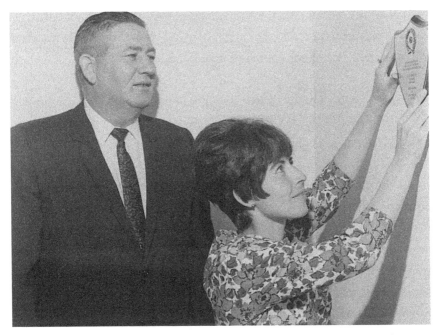

Bill Daniels served as the Texas Tech police chief from 1959 to 1986. Also shown is secretary Mary Ann Grandjean. (Courtesy the Southwest Collection, Texas Tech Public Information Collection, Bill Daniels and Mary Ann Grandjean, box 7, image 464, U148.0.)

verdict of acquittal on the grounds that the state had failed to prove Lach guilty of murder. The judge overruled the request, and after a brief recess, the defense began its case.

Gillespie first called to the witness stand Bill Daniels, chief of security at Tech. Daniels testified that several days after the murder, his office received an anonymous and so-called "crank" tape recording in the mail. The recording was then played to the jury:

> I want to make it clear that I know that I killed the old lady. . . . I didn't really mean to do it, you know? So I never know what I am going to do. I am crazy, I know that. But I am not crazy enough to walk into any cop house and tell, tell you that I did it. But I need help. I mean if you think she was bleeding you should have seen me.

Several four-letter words were scattered throughout the recording, and the person who made the tape recording breathed heavily into the microphone. One of the last audible sentences was:

> If I want to get in a fight Saturday night I can do it. And if I want to kill somebody. And so maybe all you guys ought to watch out.
>   That's all . . . all I got to tell you. That's all.

As the proceedings continued, Lucy Lach stood outside the courthouse on a Fort Worth street corner talking to reporters about her son. "I think with all my heart that he is innocent," she said. "He has written me letters saying that he is suffering from someone else's crime."

Mrs. Lach, who listened to testimony on the first day of the trial, had not been allowed back in the courtroom since then because she had been sworn in as a witness. "I don't think they will call me, I think they just didn't want me in there," she said.

While talking to reporters, Mrs. Lach clutched a sack of freshly baked cookies. "They wouldn't let me give them to him," she said.

Testifying for the defense on day four of the trial was the witness who provided an alibi for Lach. Former Tech student Joan Dominick told the court that Lach was with her at the time of the murder.

Described by a newspaper reporter as "an attractive divorcee," the twenty-nine-year-old had custody of her seven-year-old daughter. The witness stated she met Lach "quite by chance" in the Student Union about 6:30 p.m. on December 4, 1967. She said they talked, and then he walked her to her apartment about eight blocks away and stayed until about nine o'clock. Morgan was believed to have been slain between 7:30 p.m. and 8 p.m., and Dominick and Lach were together at her apartment during that time, according to Dominick.

This testimony directly conflicted with that of several other witnesses who said they had seen Lach in the Science Building about 7 p.m. that evening. The testimony of Dominick also differed from Lach's own statement of his whereabouts and actions that night.

Under cross-examination by Griffin, Dominick revealed that as a Tech student, she had written short stories, many of them dealing with mental telepathy. Griffin read aloud excerpts from one such story, which Dominick called a "fiction fantasy." In the story, which she said was based on her encounter with Lach on December 4, she calls him "a renegade telepath." She wrote in the four-page story that Lach's "mind gave off certain beeps."

Dominick wrote that she could always tell where Lach was by the beeps. She wrote that "when I beeped Ben on campus I was surprised because I thought he was at work at the cab company." Dominick submitted the short story to Dr. W. D. Miller, her geology professor, sometime after the Morgan murder, according to her testimony.

Griffin also questioned Dominick about a letter she had written to Dr. Miller on March 26, 1968. In it, Dominick wrote that "it is very important that I remember anything that I did on Monday the 4th of December 1967." She told the court that her letter was intended to ascertain what Miller had lectured on in his class; however, no mention of the lecture was made in the letter.

Next, Texas Tech senior Rita Navarro testified, saying she and five friends attended the Carol of Lights the night after the Morgan murder. Following the ceremony, she said the group walked to the third floor of the Science Building and stood outside of the room where the murder occurred, when a man approached and asked them if they wanted to go inside the locked room.

Navarro said the man, who she later learned was biology professor Dr. Francis Rose, pointed to where the body was discovered. She testified that she later identified Rose as being the man shown in one of the composite drawings during the police investigation.

Cheri Shields, a Tech graduate student and friend and roommate of Navarro, offered similar testimony. Shields related that while on a double date with an airman (and Navarro) they decided to "visit the place where it happened" at about 8 p.m. on December 5, 1967. While near the science lab where the murder occurred, the group saw a man they did not know.

"He had a very strange look on his face . . . a stare on his face," she testified. "He looked like he was looking through you."

Shields said the man unlocked the lab and told them how he believed the killer used a scalpel to cut Morgan's throat. The witness said she learned later the man was Dr. Francis Rose, and that after adding eyeglasses to a newspaper's composite drawing of a suspect, she noticed it had a strong resemblance to Rose.

Special prosecutor Alton Griffin quickly reminded Shields that Rose had provided information for the drawing.

"Do you think he would have provided information for a self-portrait?" Griffin asked.

Griffin also suggested that Shields's nervousness could have led her to conclude in error that Rose had a strange stare on his face.

Dallas psychologist Dr. Robert Glen was next called by the defense. His testimony led to a testy exchange with the prosecutor and admonishment from the judge to the witness.

Glen told the court he had examined Lach twice during the previous five weeks. According to the psychologist, Lach was a paranoid schizophrenic who could have been pressured into confessing to the murder of Alice Morgan.

The witness said Lach was raised in a home fearful of police: his parents, Herman and Lucy Lach, immigrated to the United States from Poland, where, as Jews, police intimidated them.

"He has a poor testing of reality," Glen testified.

Gillespie noted that Lach was arrested by several armed Lubbock officers, questioned for some time without an attorney present, and only afterwards made the statement implicating his involvement in the murder.

"Would you agree that he would succumb to the pressure and agree with anything they said?" Gillespie asked the witness.

"Pressure would make him much sicker," Glen replied. "He would be inclined to agree with any kind of pressure put on him. . . . He would have a tendency under pressure to agree because he was afraid, scared stiff, and because he could not fully understand the consequences of his act."

Prosecutor Griffin objected on several occasions during this line of questioning. At one point, after Griffin objected to a Gillespie query, Glen turned to Griffin and asked, "Could you give me some clue as to what is bothering you?"

Griffin then objected to the witness asking a question.

A few minutes later, Glen received a strong warning from Judge Matthews.

"I appreciate expert witnesses and expert testimony, but I will remonstrate any witness who is trying to evade, distort, or mislead a jury through his testimony," the judge told the witness.

Bart Blaydes, another defense witness who was a Tech student at the time of the crime, testified he was in the basement of the Science Building "about 7:30 to 7:45 on the night of the murder and saw a man 30 to 40 yards down the hall." He said the lights were out at the other end of the hall, but that he could see that the person had a flattop haircut. Blaydes stated he was certain the person was not Lach.

On cross-examination, Griffin read from a police report that indicated Blaydes told investigators that he left the Science Building at 7:10 p.m., to which Blaydes admitted that it was possible he left at the earlier time.

Defense witness Ron Johnson (pseudonym), a former Tech student and current schoolteacher, related how he took a polygraph test at police headquarters "a week and a half after the [December 4] mishap." He said he was told the test showed that he was "lying in a few instances" and urged to "go ahead and confess and the state will go easy on you."

Johnson said he was approached by a plainclothes police officer one day as he entered a lab in the Science Building. The officer requested that Johnson accompany him to the police station, where Johnson recalled he was "identified" from behind a one-way mirror. "The door was ajar and a woman said, 'That's him,'" Johnson said. He said he was later verbally harassed by authorities and told by an officer, "We know you did it."

During his cross-examination, Griffin asked: "But you've never been questioned again, harassed, had someone following you and never were charged, were you?"

"No, sir," Johnson replied.

The final witness of the day was Dr. Charles Moment, a mathematics teacher at Central Oklahoma State College, and a Tech student in December 1967. Moment said he overheard a conversation by two men in the Tech Student Union on December 9, 1967—five days after the fateful night. He said the two men were discussing the possibility that they wouldn't be caught "now that they had killed that old woman or some such words."

Griffin, however, produced the police report that Moment had made in December 1967, read it back to Moment, and suggested that there was no mention of "murder" or a "killing." Moment conceded there might not have been, but he maintained his contention that he understood the two men were discussing a killing.

As the final day of testimony dawned, Lubbock County District Attorney Cherry filed burglary and theft charges against the defendant—the burglary charge was in connection with the unlawful entrance into the office of Tech biology professor Dr. Kent Rylander, and the theft charge involved the automobile stolen from Judy Beavers. Both offenses occurred on March 13, 1968, the morning of Lach's arrest for murder.

Lucy Lach, the fifty-year-old mother of the defendant, was one of four witnesses to testify on the final day of the trial. She told of the extermination of her and her husband's families by the Nazis during World War II. Additionally, she described how Herman and she had moved their children from country to country in an effort to escape further persecution.

Weeping quietly for most of her fifty-five minutes on the stand, the defendant's mother recalled the horror of "dodging bombs" during World War II. A native of Latvia, she said she had lived in Russia, Poland, Estonia, Germany, and Israel.

"We had trouble surviving," she said. "No one knew I was Jewish. . . . They were looking for Jews to kill." She said she protected Benjamin by claiming to be his aunt. "He called me aunt until he was two years old," she recalled.

Mrs. Lucy Lach said Benjamin was born in Poland, and the family moved to the United States in 1959, when he was fourteen years old.

She volunteered she couldn't speak English when the family arrived in America, but that she was currently fluent in seven languages: German, Polish, Russian, Latvian, Yiddish, Hebrew, and English.

In her testimony, Mrs. Lach outlined Benjamin's schooling and background, emphasizing his participation in football, tennis, bowling, and swimming, and the fact that he had obtained a lifesaving certificate after completing a Red Cross course. She said he also served as a counselor at a youth summer camp.

Testifying in rebuttal for the state was Larry Hagood, whose family was friends with the defendant. The witness told the court Lach visited the Hagood home on at least four occasions—he said one of the visits occurred between February 8 and March 13, 1968, the period during which Lach had been administered two polygraph tests and had been examined by a psychologist.

"Did anything unusual happen on any of these visits?" Griffin asked.

Hagood said he remembered they were entertaining Lach once when Mrs. Hagood received a telephone message to call Lubbock Police Chief J. T. Alley.

"There were other people there," Hagood recalled. "There was glib talk about the police finally catching up with her [Mrs. Hagood] about running a stoplight." Hagood added that he did not notice any reaction from Lach during the conversation.

The following morning, however, Hagood said Lach called him. "I couldn't tell you last night," he quoted Lach as saying, "but it's about me. My bicycle was seen near that building where they found that woman and they were wanting to question me."

"Are they treating you all right?" Hagood asked Lach.

"Yes," Lach replied. Hagood said he asked Lach if he had an attorney and to not let "the police push you around."

Hagood said Lach told him, "They've [the police] been very nice to me. They wanted my sweater and I've given it to them."

Hagood also told the court that Lach seemed "calm and collected" when he called about the police questioning, and that he never expressed a fear of police.

In recalling his testimony years later, Hagood said, "Ben called me while he was in jail and I told him to tell the truth and not let them [police] hassle him. I made a mistake saying that—the defense jumped all over that. I didn't mean to imply that they would do anything improper in a physical way."

Later in his testimony, Hagood stated that Lach and a girlfriend from Boston spent the night with the Hagood family.

"Did he ever seem anything like other than a normal college student to you?" Griffin asked.

"No . . . no, he didn't," Hagood responded.

In an interview some thirty-five years after the trial, Hagood remembered one unusual encounter: "On one of his [Lach's] visits with us, his girlfriend came down and we went to Lake Tahoka," Hagood said. "He cut his hand—it was what we call just a country scratch—but he went berserk. He washed his hand obsessively—just over and over, you wouldn't believe how many times."

Both sides delivered closing arguments on November 7, 1970. About two dozen spectators sat in the courtroom, but only a handful remained later in the day. Throughout the trial, attendance was sparse, with court officials, attorneys, and news media comprising most of those present. No family members of victim Alice Morgan attended the proceedings.

"Alice Morgan gave her life so Benjamin Lach could make high grades," Special Prosecutor Alton Griffin told the jurors. "He was killing for his own selfish motives of not wanting anyone to know he was cheating to get high grades. . . . I submit to you that the evidence shows that Benjamin Lach killed her.

"How do you account for the fact that Benjamin Lach had a key [to Dr. Kent Rylander's office] when only 37 had been issued in five years and all of them were accounted for but this one?" Griffin asked, holding up a small envelope in front of the jury. "And why would he run? Why would he run 38 blocks . . . steal a car . . . then stop and tell an officer, 'I'm not gonna be taken alive' just for breaking and entering?

"The motive?" Griffin continued. "Well, I grant you that it [key] wasn't enough to kill Alice Morgan for—but he did. Benjamin Lach wasn't the one lying on the floor in room 304-J . . . with his throat cut . . . with his spinal column cut almost two inches. . . . He cut in slashes. Benjamin Lach wanted to be a doctor, so he cut it in slashes. This is the kind of individual that society cannot afford to have on the streets of Tarrant County, Lubbock County, or Boston."

District Attorney Blair Cherry had opened the prosecution's final arguments, stating that "if you don't find him guilty, you'll be turning a killer loose on society. This man is guilty. I ask you to find him guilty."

Countering the state's claims was defense attorney Bill Gillespie in his closing argument.

"When Blair Cherry says you're going to turn a killer loose on society, you weigh that. . . . You just weigh that. Look right down the wire in every instance at the logic of this case and look at the failure of the prosecution to prove beyond reasonable doubt. When you [the jury] does [*sic*] this," Gillespie continued, "the scales of justice will tip one way—to the side of the defendant."

In his closing comments, defense co-counsel A. W. Salyars said the state had four key points:

1. That the defendant went into Dr. Rylander's office. "But that doesn't prove murder."
2. The key. "Hers was missing. He had one. That's not beyond reasonable doubt."
3. Identification. "Not proven beyond reasonable doubt."
4. The confession. "There is no mention of a saw. But he did say, 'I don't remember doing it.'"

Salyars also reminded the jury of the "third-party confession" mailed to Tech Security by an unknown person. "He [the speaker on the tape] said they'll never catch him, and knowing the Lubbock Police Department, I'm not surprised."

Also mentioning the tape in his closing statement was defense team member Dawson Davis:

> Thank God for that recording—for that tape. You can't find one scintilla of evidence that points to this boy (Lach) except that some people saw him in the Science Building. This boy was trying to get some examination questions (that's the very slightest motive, and who hasn't cheated a little bit?). That's the only motive they could possibly have.

Finally, Gillespie said the state "never connected one thing to Ben." He said a shirt, size 15 1/2-34, which was sent to the FBI, was not linked to the defendant. But he pointed out that one prosecution witness, a Tech professor, testified that he didn't know his shirt size.

"There is more proof against Dr. [Francis] Rose by far than there is against this young man," Salyars said, pointing at Lach and reminding the jury that the murder took place in Rose's lab, with his scalpel, and with only his fingerprints at the scene.

Alluding to the fact that the defense had pointed an accusing finger at Rose and others, Griffin said, "If you don't have a defense, try somebody else."

The jury began their deliberations at 1:24 p.m. During this time, Lucy Lach sat alone on a bench in the courtroom and talked to reporters. "If there is justice in this country, my boy will be called innocent and I can take him home with me," Mrs. Lach said. "I talked with him yesterday," she continued, "and he told me he is innocent. He has never once lied to me in his life. He would have no reason to lie to me now for I am not his judge. I believe him. He never drank. Never smoked. Studied hard always. He worked hard also. He was like a father to his brother and sister and they loved him like one. He is kind. He could never kill."

Smoothing out a wrinkle on her bright blue gabardine dress, Mrs. Lach said: "He was a boy born at a bad time in history. . . . I can say no more to you now. In some countries there is no justice. I hope there is justice in this country. But I wait to see. My son is innocent. He told me."

Rylander, in a 2004 interview, recalled an awkward encounter with Mrs. Lach. "I was out in the hall and then his mother came up to me before I was on the stand. She knew who I was, I guess, and she said, 'You know, I didn't have any murderers. All my children are just angels. They wouldn't do anything to hurt,' and she started crying."

One newspaper account described Benjamin Lach's demeanor as follows: "The curly-haired defendant listened intently to testimony throughout the trial and sometimes wrote notes to his lawyers. But, when held in a cell near the courtroom during recesses, he alternately whistled gay tunes and scrubbed on the bars with scraps of tissue."

After a trial that had lasted nineteen days, the jury needed only one hour and fifty-eight minutes to reach its decision—the verdict was returned at 3:22 p.m.

SIDEBAR: THE CASE OF THE MISSING KEYS AND FOOTBALL

From a historical perspective, this was not the first time that stolen keys had created controversy at Texas Tech, albeit of a less serious nature. According to *Evolution of a University: Texas Tech's First Fifty Years* (1975) by Jane Gilmore Rushing and Kline Nall:

> In 1957–1958 the college had what was probably its most celebrated discipline matter, which became known as "the key ring case." A foreign student, a brilliant Greek male, impelled by a desire to be of help to the football team, obtained master keys to practically every office on campus—made easier by obtaining first a master key to the locksmith's office. He then helped players by furnishing copies of

professors' exams. The most memorable event from this entire episode was the placing on probation of an important football player. For the player, and for interested football fans, especially downtown quarterbacks, this was equivalent to disaster. Pressures caused the president, Dr. E. N. Jones, to ask for reconsideration of the matter. Again the Discipline Committee recommended probation, and President Jones, for the time, accepted the recommendation. He succumbed to pressure, however, and his letter removing the young man from probation was mailed the morning he and Mrs. Jones left for a two-month trip to Europe. Jones's stock with the faculty fell appreciably.

Although the book provides an insightful, historical account of the university, curiously enough it makes no mention of the Alice Morgan murder.

CHAPTER 8

THE VERDICT

MANY TIMES, AT THE END OF A LONG, hard-fought criminal trial, tension fills the air of a courtroom and pent-up emotions are released when a verdict is announced. But that wasn't about to happen when Judge Byron Matthews was in charge.

When the bailiff escorted Benjamin Lach back into Tarrant County Criminal District Court No. 1 to hear the jury's verdict, the defendant had a smile on his face. Judge Matthews sternly issued a warning to the courtroom spectators: "I trust we won't have any outbreaks when this verdict is read. If anyone feels he cannot control his emotions, please leave the courtroom now."

The smile on the defendant's face disappeared as the judge read the following verdict:

"We the jury find the defendant guilty as charged in the indictment."

Lach showed little emotion, while his mother sat motionless, staring straight ahead, her eyes still red from weeping during final arguments. Not a tear trickled down her high cheekbones. A friend seated beside whispered a word of comfort; Mrs. Lach had no public comment but twisted a pair of colored glasses from hand to hand.

The state sought the death penalty, while the defense requested the minimum of two years in prison; neither side offered evidence on the issue of punishment.

And just forty-eight minutes later, the jury returned its decision regarding punishment. As the courtroom again fell quiet, Lach stared at a paper on the defense counsel table and didn't look up until his attorneys stood.

The jury set Lach's sentence at forty years but failed to complete the wording of the verdict on the punishment issue. This omission prompted Judge Matthews to ask the jurors if he could add the words "in the penitentiary" to the written verdict. They responded "yes," and the judge advised the state and defense that he was adding the additional wording.

After announcing the punishment, Judge Matthews said, "I want to thank the lawyers in this case for their diligence to both sides and the courtesies they have extended the court in the trial of this case. I have never had a case harder fought but more courteously done. I appreciate the ability and courteous treatment that the court received in the trial. I want to thank the press. I feel I have never seen the press restrain themselves more completely in reporting the facts in the case and yet not doing anything that would attempt to keep this defendant from receiving a fair trial in this county. You have my personal thanks for that, Gentlemen."

Special Prosecutor Griffin addressed the jurors afterward, telling them, "We felt the facts in this case justify the [death] penalty. But so long as you can look yourself in the eye and know you have done the correct thing, then no one will question your decision." Later, he said that if the penalty were not death for "the man who committed this murder, the penalty should be confinement for the rest of his life."

Lucy Lach saw it differently, however. "Justice has not been served," she said. "I talked to my son yesterday and he said he was innocent."

Years later, DA Cherry reflected on the verdict. "I was somewhat disappointed that the jury did not give him life," he said. "The death penalty in Texas at the time was under attack and was soon to be declared unconstitutional, so I was not disappointed that he was not given the

The University Daily, student newspaper at Texas Tech, headlines a story detailing the conviction of Benjamin Lach. (Courtesy the Southwest Collection, *University Daily* 46, no. 47.)

death penalty. I did think that, given his offense and his prior history, he should have had to face a capital trial. We got the jury's verdict of guilt around 4 p.m. on a Saturday, the 19th day of trial, and Judge Byron Matthews, who was a very fine trial judge, insisted on proceeding with the punishment stage at that time, rather than waiting until Monday morning as we had requested. Given that, it was not really surprising that we got the forty-year sentence."

"I didn't expect the death penalty," Griffin said, when looking back at the decision thirty-five years later. "I thought there was no way he would get the death penalty after he had been sent to Rusk [State Hospital]."

In 1972, the death penalty was outlawed when the US Supreme Court declared capital punishment cruel and unusual because of its arbitrary nature. The following year, the Texas Legislature revised the state's penal code to address the court's concerns; in 1974, the death penalty was reinstated in Texas.

At least one witness involved in the proceedings was less than enamored with the process.

"That trial almost destroyed my faith in our judicial system," said Dr. Kent Rylander, who had been in South America on sabbatical but returned to testify. "It got very ugly, and I recall that he [defense attorney] tried to belittle me before the jury by making fun of the fact that I didn't know my [shirt] collar size. Beginning professors couldn't afford shirts, which, at that time, had collar sizes—we just bought medium shirts! Moreover, he [attorney] held up a piece of paper he claimed said that the Key Shop at Tech had issued me a master key to the building when I began working for Tech. The implication was that master keys were commonly issued to people who worked in the building, so the one found on Ben Lach didn't signify anything important. When I later indicated to District Attorney Blair Cherry my amazement that the Key Shop had incorrectly listed me as having a master key, instead of the sub-master key to our floors only that the faculty were given, Mr. Cherry said that the defense attorney was holding a blank piece of paper instead of a document from the Key Shop. Why Mr. Cherry didn't object at the moment to prevent the jury from accepting incorrect information surprised me."

SIDEBAR: THE LUBBOCK TORNADO

Just six months prior to the start of the Benjamin Lach murder trial, Lubbock received a brutal kick from Mother Nature.

On Monday, May 11, 1970, a deadly tornado ripped across downtown, devastating parts of the city. The twister left twenty-six people dead, injured 500, and caused $150 million in property damage. The vicious storm ravaged twenty-five square miles in the city, destroying 430 homes and leaving 1,800 people homeless.

The *Avalanche-Journal* newspaper building on Avenue J was among the damaged businesses, and the next morning's edition was printed by the *Amarillo Globe-News*. The funnel bounced across the Tech campus, hitting an area just east of the school, and ultimately moved downtown and beyond. The light standards on the east side of Tech's Jones Stadium were bent in half by the storm.

In the aftermath of the tornado, Tech's commencement ceremony, scheduled for May 15 in the Lubbock Municipal Coliseum, was cancelled, with graduates receiving their diplomas in the mail. Thirty years later, the Office of the Provost and the Ex-Students Association offered those 1970 graduates a formal graduation ceremony in conjunction with the summer 2000 commencement ceremony.

The city recovered from the tornado, in great part, due to the leadership of Lubbock mayor James Granberry.

CHAPTER 9

THE COURT OF APPEALS

THREE DAYS AFTER HIS CONVICTION, ON NOVEMBER 10, 1970, Benjamin Lach's attorneys waived his right to appeal, and Judge Matthews formally pronounced sentence, granting a defense request to award Lach credit for the time he had already spent in jail awaiting trial and for time served at Rusk State Hospital since his arrest on March 13, 1968. With the right to appeal waived, District Attorney Cherry recommended the burglary and auto theft charges still pending against Lach be dropped.

The legal process is never as simple as it seems, however. By all indications, Lach was set to begin his prison term, while the court and attorneys could turn their attention to other cases.

But not so fast.

Less than a month after waiving the appeal, Lach changed his mind. Thus began a tedious and lengthy series of appeals and legal maneuvering.

Cherry disclosed to reporters that he had been contacted by a Houston attorney "who informed me that he had been hired by some

Houston attorney Carl Dally was involved in filing numerous appeals for convicted murderer Benjamin Lach. Dally later became a judge on the Texas Court of Criminal Appeals. (Author collection.)

people from the East to represent Lach in an attempt to appeal his conviction of murder with malice."

Carl Dally, a forty-six-year-old Houston attorney, was retained by the convicted killer's family to work on Lach's appeal. Dally served as assistant district attorney of Harris County from 1960 until 1966, when he became a partner in the Houston law firm of Briscoe, Dally and Shaffer.

"The law provides that a defendant must give notice of appeal within 10 days from the date of conviction," he said. "Of course, the time period has lapsed, but the judge has the right to grant a late appeal." Dally said that if his motion to appeal failed, he might make a "collateral attack" on the judgment by filing a writ of habeas corpus, which would order Lach be brought before the judge to determine whether he was imprisoned lawfully and if he should be released should it be determined that a legal error had been made.

Countered Cherry: "Since Lach signed a written waiver of appeal, any attempt to appeal will be vigorously resisted by our office. If the appeal is denied, Lach will have to pursue the matter by way of writ of habeas corpus. Although the appeal on hearings of habeas corpus will be quite time-consuming, I am confident that there is no reversible error in the case."

Cherry added that he would also seek indictments in the two previously dismissed cases (burglary and auto theft) against Lach when the next grand jury convened in January 1971.

The appeals process began on December 3, 1970, when Dally and co-counsel Joe Shaffer filed a motion requesting that Lach's forty-year sentence be vacated in order for their client to file a late notice of appeal and a motion for a new trial.

Both attorneys were former lawyers from the Harris County District Attorney's Office. Dally, a native of Denver, Colorado, graduated from the University of Denver Law School and was admitted to the Texas Bar in 1954, while Shaffer graduated from the University of Houston Law Center in 1960.

Lach's new attorneys claimed in their appeal that at the time he was sentenced, provisions set down by the Texas Code of Criminal Procedure were not followed. They further argued his court-appointed defense attorneys pressured Lach to waive his right to appeal.

"The defendant has been represented by his court-appointed attorneys for almost three years," the appeal read. "He is truly appreciative of their efforts in his behalf. He has wholly, totally, relied upon them for advice and counsel throughout all of the preparations for and litigation up until the time he was sentenced."

Dally and Shaffer said the two court-appointed attorneys—Bill Gillespie and A. W. Salyars—visited Lach prior to formal sentencing and "advised and urged" him to immediately accept the sentence.

"They told him that he was fortunate to have received only 40 years and not to have received the death penalty," according to the petition. "They further urged him to go immediately to the penitentiary and cause no trouble. They assured him that they would intercede for him with the Board of Pardons and Paroles and the governor, and that he would serve his time and be released."

According to the new counsel, Lach was "in a state of shock and of disbelief that a jury could have found him guilty of the crime which he still now steadfastly denies he committed.

"While in such a state of shock and under the strong and overpowering influence of his court-appointed attorneys, the defendant, against his will, was persuaded and prevailed upon to accept immediate sentence and in haste he was sentenced without the filing of a motion for new trial and without giving notice of appeal."

"I never understood the consequences of my signing a waiver," Lach said, adding that he never had the opportunity to talk to his mother about an appeal.

The relentless appeals attorneys requested that Judge Byron Matthews set a date for a hearing and issue a bench warrant in order for Lach to testify. Judge Matthews told the *A-J* that he would consider the motions, "but unless something is proven to me other than that which I already know about, I will not permit the case to be reopened under any circumstances. I will talk to Lubbock's District Attorney [Cherry] before

I make any definite plans. But right now, I would be in a frame of mind to deny any kind of hearing."

As expected, the judge formally denied the motion to vacate Lach's sentence on December 17, 1970—that prompted the Dally-Shaffer team to file another motion that the forty-year term be set aside. The new motion contended Judge Matthews did not have authority to sentence Lach before a ten-day period had passed. Matthews also denied that motion.

Dally was not finished, however. On April 15, 1971, he filed a lengthy habeas corpus motion that again asserted Judge Matthews did not have the authority to impose sentence and that Lach did not "knowingly" waive his right to a ten-day appeal period at the conclusion of the trial. The motion also asserted that the sentence should be set aside due to Lach's mental state when he signed the waiver of his rights. It contended that Lach was "under intimidation, duress and coercion" at the time. Dally also stated in the brief that Lach's court-appointed attorneys— Gillespie and Salyars—did not effectively represent the defendant during the trial.

One Tarrant County Assistant DA—John Brady—termed it "the most voluminous writ of habeas corpus I have ever seen."

A hearing on the matter was held on July 22, 1971, in Fort Worth, with Judge Matthews again presiding, Dally representing Lach, and Cherry, Griffin, and Brady arguing on behalf of the state. Bill Gillespie and A. W. Salyars, Lach's original court-appointed trial attorneys, testified at the hearing that they conferred with their client on three different occasions following the jury's guilty verdict and prior to sentencing.

On August 2, 1971, Judge Matthews denied the latest motion by Dally.

"It is the conclusion of this court that the defendant intelligently waived his right of appeal . . . and received able, conscientious and successful representation by his court-appointed attorneys during all phases of his trial and subsequent to the trial and at the time he was sentenced," Matthews said in a written finding of fact. The judge stated that Lach "was very ably represented by counsel and there is absolutely no merit in this contention that he did not have adequate representation during the trial, during the sentencing, and at the time he waived his appeal."

The judge said that if he granted the motion, "the court would be opening the door to many frivolous and unconscionable motions and appeals."

Undaunted, Dally and Shaffer filed yet another motion, again contending that Lach was "in a state of shock" at the time he waived his appeal. Judge Matthews indicated that he would hold a hearing on the new motion within the next month.

Although Benjamin Lach was one of some 15,000 Texas prison inmates, the bizarre case remained in the news from time to time.

In March 1971, United Press International (UPI) reported that the Lubbock District Attorney's Office was investigating an incident in which Texas Tech biology professor Dr. Kent Rylander received a badly mutilated baby doll in the mail. DA Blair Cherry told UPI his office was in possession of the doll and the box in which it was mailed. He said the package, postmarked in Lubbock on February 16, 1971, was wrapped in a plain brown cover and contained a fictitious return address. Rylander had assisted authorities in the Alice Morgan murder investigation and testified at the Lach trial.

"I don't think anything about it—it just came," Rylander said. "It was probably some kind of prank. But it's sort of stupid to speculate on something like this."

It was later reported that Joan Dominick, a Lach defense witness, was responsible for sending the package. She continued to harass Rylander for quite some time, even visiting his office on one occasion. Dominick eventually apologized to Rylander for her actions.

Incredibly enough, on January 12, 1972, another murder occurred in the Science Building. According to Associated Press (AP) accounts, fifty-seven-year-old Julian Sanchez Ramos, a Tech custodian, confessed to the shooting deaths of female janitor Manuela Constancio, age forty-five, and Tech graduate student/teaching assistant Michael Clingan, age twenty-nine.

Shortly before 9 p.m., four people watched helplessly as Ramos, after waxing a floor in the basement of the Science Building, shot the two victims in the back and head. The four witnesses, all members of the custodial staff, said Constancio and Clingan were talking as the gunman stepped through a doorway and started shooting. Police officers said they found a .38 caliber pistol atop a cabinet in a room near where the bodies lay in the southeast corner of the hallway, and Ramos was taken into custody at the scene.

Clingan was pursuing a master's degree in physics at the time, and part of his duties as a teaching assistant were to teach two undergraduate physics labs. He had also been conducting experiments and doing research.

The science professors did not want custodians moving expensive equipment in the lab, so they would work with the staff to pick a convenient day for cleaning. It was common practice for professors and graduate assistants to move the lab equipment themselves. And on that fateful night, Clingan and Professor Glenn Mann had done just that, moving furniture and equipment into the hallway to allow the custodians to thoroughly clean the floor. Dr. Mann and Clingan planned to meet at nine o'clock to move the contents back into the lab.

In his confession, Ramos told police he saw the two victims talking and "heard voices" telling him they were plotting to kill him.

Ramos was determined to be insane and sent to Rusk State Hospital. But four years later, he was diagnosed as sane and sent back to Lubbock to stand trial for murder with malice. After being convicted in 1977, Ramos received a fifty-year prison sentence.

Authorities discovered that he had been committed to Big Spring State Hospital on three previous occasions. Ramos first worked as a Tech custodian from May 1966 until September 1967 before being hospitalized; he was rehired as a custodian on September 24, 1970.

Ironically, in the early days of the Alice Morgan murder investigation, Ramos's name surfaced as that of a possible suspect. However, investigators determined Ramos was confined in the Big Spring hospital at the time of the murder. The 1972 slaying was the fourth tragedy to occur in a Tech building during a span of just six years: In 1967, of course, was the Morgan murder; in 1968, a Tech student jumped nine floors to his death from the Biology Building (then under construction just north-west of the Science Building); and, in 1971, a fifteen-year-old Lubbock youth fell ten stories to his death in the elevator shaft of the new Business Administration Building (southwest of the Science Building). All these horrific events took place in close proximity to one another on campus.

SIDEBAR: TEXAS LEGISLATURE "HONORS" BOSTON STRANGLER

In 1971, Texas lawmakers unanimously passed a bill honoring Albert DeSalvo, better known as the Boston Strangler.

On April 1, 1971, Rep. Tom Moore Jr. introduced a resolution in the Texas House of Representatives commending DeSalvo for his "unconventional techniques involving population control and applied psychology."

Moore knew his fellow legislators often passed bills without fully reading or understanding them. As expected, the resolution passed unanimously, and Moore immediately withdrew the resolution and explained that he was just trying to prove a point.

SIDEBAR: TIMOTHY COLE AND A CASE OF MISTAKEN IDENTITY

In late 1984 and into early 1985, Lubbock police sought to arrest an unknown person referred to as the "Texas Tech rapist." During that time, at least five violent rapes occurred near the Tech campus.

Timothy Brian Cole, an African American military veteran and Tech student, was eventually arrested in connection with the rape of a twenty-year-old student at the university.

In 1986, Cole was convicted of aggravated sexual assault in a jury trial, primarily based on the testimony of the victim. He was sentenced to twenty-five years in prison.

Nine years later, in 1995, another man confessed to the crime. The victim later admitted that she was mistaken as to the identity of her attacker. In addition, DNA evidence showed Cole to be innocent.

Cole died in prison on December 2, 1999, during an asthma attack. His family and the victim, through the Innocence Project of Texas, sought to clear his name.

In 2009, a Texas district court judge exonerated Cole of the crime, which led to numerous changes in Texas law.

On March 1, 2010, Gov. Rick Perry granted Timothy Cole the state's first posthumous pardon.

In 2015, the Texas Tech Board of Regents awarded Cole posthumously an honorary degree in law and social justice. The City of Lubbock created the Timothy Cole Memorial Park and established a plaque in his honor.

CHAPTER 10

A MODEL PRISONER

LUBBOCK AVALANCHE-JOURNAL JOURNALIST Dave Knapp's persistence and determination in covering the Alice Morgan murder case did not cease with the arrest, conviction, and imprisonment of Benjamin Lach. Six years into Lach's prison term, Knapp, by then the executive editor of the *A-J*, traveled the 466 miles to Huntsville, Texas, home of the Texas prison system.

Huntsville, located about an hour's drive north of Houston, is also the site of Sam Houston State University, an institution known for its outstanding criminal justice program. Legendary TV newsman Dan Rather is the school's most notable alumnus.

Knapp's extensive prison interview with Inmate No. 213519 was published in the April 18, 1976, edition of the *A-J*, and the timing of the article coincided with the expectation of Lach's parole hearing in the near future. A sidebar to Knapp's interview noted that "Lach has been the model prisoner many officials thought he would be when he was convicted of murder and sentenced to 40 years in the state prison."

By definition, a "model" prisoner would likely be someone who exhibited good behavior, stayed out of trouble (no disciplinary issues), functioned well while incarcerated, furthered their education, showed personal growth, and set goals.

The sidebar continued:

Assigned to the Eastham, Ramsey and Walls units of the Texas Department of Corrections, Lach has no disciplinary problems since he was incarcerated in November, 1970. He worked in the field at Eastham for approximately one year and earned an associate of applied science degree in business, maintaining a 3.4 average.

In addition, he was active in the Eastham Sunday school class, serving as a teacher. Later he finished one semester of college credit while working as a bookkeeper in the education department and furniture factory.

At the Walls unit, Lach participated in a college program and is listed as a graduate student at Sam Houston State University with a major in psychology. He also has been accepted as a graduate student at the University of Houston, with a major in behavioral science, and has made application to the Boston University School of Public Communications. He hopes to be paroled to Boston.

In addition to being the editor of *The Echo*, the nation's No. 1 penal newspaper, Lach also is a corps member of the transactional analysis program at Huntsville. He has been a Class III trusty since October 1971, and is an honorary Jaycee in the Huntsville Junior Chamber of Commerce.

He also was administered the Birkman Psychological Personality Evaluation test, which indicated:

- Getting along with others: Ability to view people in a matter-of-fact way and to deal with others in a direct and objective manner.
- Giving and accepting direction: Ability to adjust comfortably to different types of authority and organizational requirements.
- Handling conflict and competition: A tendency to reason factually, to think in practical and competitive terms.

- Emotional and physical stamina: A personal courage and strength of which will enable him to achieve goals which require high standards of perseverance.
- Organizing and planning: A basic optimism and ability to take positive action and to venture from the tried and proven.
- Decision-making: A greater-than-average liking for the new and adventurous.

Knapp's one-on-one interview with Lach was, at times, revealing:

"Tech Slayer Lach Eager for Parole"
By Dave Knapp, Executive Editor
HUNTSVILLE—The ivy has climbed the red brick walls of the state penitentiary here.

Bluebonnets, blooming in profusion, dot the landscape. You admire the scenery.

Suddenly, you are jolted back to reality as an armed guard strides across the wall of "The Slammer." You continue toward the entrance, walking briskly through a heavy shower. It's spring—and the season may mean a new life for a convicted killer you are here to interview.

You climb the stairs and wait for the bars to slide open. Once inside you walk through a metal-detecting electronic device and surrender your briefcase for scrutiny.

A guard tells you to sign in; then he hands you a "Visitor" badge. "You've got to wear it," he says with a grin. You look toward the "bullring" where your interview will be conducted. You are impressed by the highly waxed tile floors and the glistening brass on the bars of the bullring. Suddenly, the man you are here to see appears on the other side of the room. A guard lets him into the building. There is little emotion on his face.

You shake hands with Benjamin Lach, convicted of the December 4, 1967, scalpel slaying of Mrs. Sarah Alice Morgan in Room 304-J of the Science Building on the Texas Tech campus. He is cordial and there is a trace of a smile. He hands you copies of the January, February, and March editions of *The Echo*, the prison's monthly newspaper. He has been the editor of the tabloid since December 1974. Last year, the paper was judged No. 1 in the American Penal Press Contest. Lach is proud of that . . . but you don't learn that until later.

You discover there are no electrical outlets in the bullring. A guard goes for a long extension cord so you can crank up your tape recorder. Meanwhile, you converse with Joe C. Shaffer of Houston, Lach's attorney, and Mrs. Gail Monroe, coordinator of public information for the Texas Department of Corrections, both of whom are going to listen to the interview. You wonder what Lach is thinking and how the interview will go. You asked for the session because Lach is up for parole this month and you don't think he is ready for release. His attorney knows how you feel; but you are concerned how Lach will react directly to the question. So you get to the point . . .

"You are coming up for parole and I requested to come and visit with you because I am not so sure you are rehabilitated.

"I am not going to ask you any questions about the case because it is still on appeal; but I will get close to it. Mainly, the questions will be confined to your rehabilitation. Okay?"

"Yes, sir, I understand," he said with a nod.

Shaffer cautions his client to "at least get a nod from me before you answer any question . . . there may be some that I would just not want you to answer. I want to reserve the right to do that since the case is on appeal."

Clean-shaven and wearing a spotless, white uniform, Lach appears confident. You get the impression early that he is "a big man on campus." So you ask him about his rehabilitation and what it consists of . . . is he ready for a return to society?

"It consists of becoming involved in a program actually taking action that will show that you are involved," he replied. "Rehabilitation is available in the prison system but it is not forced upon you. So, each person that goes through a period of incarceration has the choice of showing his improvement and rehabilitation by taking on responsibilities, proving that when he is assigned certain jobs he is able to carry them out.

"There are a number of activities in which one can participate . . . for example, you have this schooling system. Those who don't have any education at all go through a lower education; those that have a college education continue education in a college program and I have done that.

"The program has social activities, such as the Jaycees. I have become involved in the Jaycees to the extent that I have become an honorary member. They have a transactional analysis group here—a study group—and I have become a member of it and it has become quite extensive in its studies and is spreading throughout the system, especially in this unit (Walls) . . . we have a pilot program here."

Lach's responses come freely. It's almost like he practiced. Your note-taking seems to annoy him. But he continues as he watches you scribble . . .

"One of the main points of rehabilitation, I feel, is the job that you are given. For example, I was given my first job—what they call a regular job assignment—as bookkeeper for the maintenance department.

"I did it well. The person that was supervising over me was satisfied with me. I have done probably the best job there. Following my stay at Eastham (another TDC unit) I transferred to the Ramsey unit for the purpose of going to the four-year college program because Eastham didn't have a four-year college.

"Ramsey is a little different than any other unit. I joined the college program out there and I was a bookkeeper in the education department. I have done my job well," he said, tugging on his ear and scratching his head.

Still looking at the notes, he adds: "If you are given a job and they tell you, 'Okay, here's a job,' nobody is going to stand there and force you to do it. And if you carry it out to the satisfaction that the job asks for, then that is meeting your responsibility.

"Becoming involved where people can depend on you is a form of rehabilitation," he added. "My first encounter with the Walls unit was when I was asked to come here and take over as editor."

Lach said he was asked to assume the new duties because he had "some experience as a reporter" when he was in the Eastham unit. He said the "administration" urged him to take the job.

Asked how the rehabilitation process has helped him overall, he noted:

"Well, I find that by being here I have learned a lot about myself. I have learned to become less hasty and to become less spontaneous than I have been. I have learned to take my time in doing any job that I have. I have learned values that before I didn't consider to be so valuable. Things that I felt were very critical before I came here, I found that they could wait and be done in longer times."

What do you mean, things very critical?

Seemingly searching for an answer, Lach rubbed his head, blinked his eyes and paused. Then he said, "For example, certain accomplishments. I felt that for a time you can accomplish anything that you set your goals at. I feel that being in prison gives you a lot of time to think about your personality, your method of achieving anything that you set your mind to do."

He said he enjoys working with people and being of "some service."

"I feel that now I have learned my journalism and I still have a long way to go but this is a field that I would like to go into."

Why?

"It enables me to—if a person is able to relay news to the average person—I feel that I know what news is important and what news is not and would be significant to the reader. Being able to select news from assorted news is important and I feel that I have that quality and can do it."

Being editor of *The Echo* is a full-time job for Lach. Monday through Friday he works from 7 a.m. to 11 a.m.; has a lunch break from 11 to 12:45 p.m. and goes back to work until 4 p.m.

He has his third meal of the day—if he chooses—at 4:30 p.m.

"I get up in the morning at 5:30—breakfast time. It's not mandatory that I get up at 5:30. If I don't get up, I don't eat breakfast. But I do get up and at 7 go to work."

He goes to college on Monday and Thursday nights from 7 p.m. until 9 p.m.; works in the crafts shop on Tuesday night; and attends the TA (transactional analysis) session on Wednesday nights. Movies are shown Friday and Saturday nights. Lach said the TA group has about fifty members.

"We have a core group of which I am a member. Our aim is to someday be an intermediate group of inmates which would work with the psychological services here and help the general population in whatever general counseling may come up. We also inject other areas of psychology that will be relevant to the form of transactional analysis," he said.

Although Lach claims to have never drank, he joined Alcoholics Anonymous at the Eastham unit to "occupy my time. I mostly joined a church program like that as a form of rehabilitation."

Do you still have aspirations of being a doctor?

"No, I don't," he said.

The question appeared to annoy him. He stared straight ahead.

What happened to that?

"Well, because of my incarceration and long stay away from scientific studies, I feel that it really held me back from continuing that career. My experience here, I feel, would be more suited toward a social service type area rather than a rigorous type medical career."

Lach said he hears from his family [in Massachusetts] "every day. I get letters every day. I write them every day. They all look forward to me getting out."

Lach said he hoped his appeal would be successful, but he admitted, "I don't know at this time."

Turning to *The Echo* again, Lach mentioned that the previous two editors of the newspaper had been paroled.

Are you just trying to follow in their footsteps? Is this a place where you have seen that the guys who have been editors of *The Echo* have gotten paroles?

"No."

You are genuinely interested in journalism?

"I am interested in journalism. In fact, I had no knowledge of journalism before I got the job and what paybacks or rewards I am able to get out of the job are really secondary.

"I feel that getting the immediate results and my immediate education in journalism is more beneficial to me. If I get any other side rewards, that would be coincidental to me. As for past editors, I am aware they have been successful in the parole program, but I don't feel that it has anything to do with me personally. Although, as editor I am trying to do my best job and hope that it will lead me to a position that I will be able to pursue when I get out."

If you were a member of the parole board, would you free a person accused of murder in such a short time in view of the number of years he received? Lach has served more than eight years, including 1 1/2 in Rusk (a mental institution for the criminally insane).

"If I knew the person and if he happened to be a person such as I am, I would."

Why do you say that?

"Because I feel that as far as time—doing time—that enough time has been done. I feel that in my individual time here I have gone all the way from the bottom, as far as inmates are concerned, to relatively the top of proving myself to be worthy of each position I have been given. I think my attitude is a healthy one . . . that I will be a productive citizen upon my release and I think that attitude is pretty important."

Informed that there was opposition—particularly in Lubbock—to his receiving a parole, he said he was surprised.

"If I had known there was that much opposition, I wouldn't mind going back to Lubbock. Nobody is my enemy out there," he added.

You were sufficiently successful on the lie detector tests and truth serum; is this a grand scheme on your part to be a nice guy and obey the rules, or are you really rehabilitated?

"Well, let me first say that I wasn't successful on those tests, I think I was telling the truth," he said, somewhat irritated. "This is regarding the lie detector tests and truth serum test."

The doors clanged in the bullring.

"As far as my subsequent action here I feel that I have gone through quite a bit of rehabilitation. I do feel that I've changed a lot from my previous behavior. I think that I've learned a lot from my experience in prison. The fact that my goals have changed, my needs and wants have changed quite a bit, I think that's another factor that, uh, would prove that I did change, despite whatever happened in the past."

How do you think you can make a contribution to society?

"Well, I think that further study in journalism, becoming more equipped with journalistic ability, I feel that I would be able to contribute as a journalist in whatever form I will pursue. I feel that my experiences here and my intentions of hoping that some of the things that some people do that leads them into crime or to the penitentiary, I will be in a position to avert a lot of that by getting into a position of counseling and being an adviser in some capacity."

Lach said he also intended to write some memoirs or possibly write a book about his experiences. "This may be a contribution," he noted. "My release will further enhance my mobility and my access to more people rather than be limited."

He said he might write more than one book. One he said, would tell it all.

Another would be about his experiences in prison. He said, "You could write a whole book about one day in the penitentiary."

He said he could go into detail on "characters, developing characters, developing activities that maybe are trivial to most people but seem to be very important to people in here because that's all they have."

Do you feel society owes you anything?

"No."

The doors clanged again, virtually drowning out his answer.

All of the psychologists and psychiatrists who examined you agreed that you would be a "model prisoner." Yet, all agreed further that if you were paroled, then were placed under a stress situation on the outside, that you might also become violent again. What is your reaction to this assessment? Is it valid?

"I don't think so. I think that psychology or psychiatry is a human behavioral course that is interpreted by individuals. They may have their right to their interpretation. Through my studying of transactional analysis I have learned about scripts. And although they may feel that I have a certain script that I may follow or will follow, I feel there is a counter-script. It's up to the individual to determine his destiny. I think that, ah, under stress situations I would, ah, I wouldn't react violently or wouldn't react in any way that would be harmful to society."

You were termed a schizophrenic individual. Were you? Are you?

"I don't think I was. I am not now."

It has gotten back through the grapevine that you, during your incarceration, compiled a list of people you were going to take care of, supposedly, when you got out. Is this true?

"No, sir," he said after glancing at his attorney, then looking directly at the others in the session. "In fact, I've got some good memories in Texas. A lot of people were my friends. I would like to pursue some of the friendships I have developed in Texas . . . but I do intend to leave Texas."

Lach has asked to be paroled to his home state of Massachusetts, where he has been promised a job in a bank. He would rather pursue a journalism degree and has applied for entry into Boston University, where he will study public communications. "I'd like to get a job in journalism on a part-time basis and was wondering if you had any connections up there?" Lach said he wouldn't mind starting at the bottom on the *Boston Globe*, which he termed "a good newspaper."

Benjamin Lach (right) poses with a friend at the Texas Prison Rodeo in Huntsville. (Author collection.)

Lach said he had managed to save some money working in the crafts shops, where he makes western belt buckles. He sold eight "last month for $25 to $30 apiece" and has saved about $300. He plans to buy a camera when he gets out to help him in his journalism career.

"I'm not bragging about it, I'm just stating a fact, but I'm the best metalworker here."

Why don't you take up metalworking?

"Well, it's not as creative. I'll probably engage in it on a part-time basis, as a hobby, but that's about all."

He said he also learned how to weld while in prison. "That came in handy when I worked metal."

Lach said he wasn't happy with the results of his trial in Fort Worth, where a jury assessed him 40 years in prison.

Lach said he hoped his release would come soon and "my actions will speak for themselves. I feel that I have gained a lot of valuable experience in here and I feel confident that I will be a productive person when I get out and my expedient release will benefit me and society."

Benjamin Lach (above center) at the prison rodeo. (Author collection.)

Editor Wins Levi's

By RICHARD UPTON
Walls Unit

Levi Strauss & Co. and the International Rodeo Writers Association (IRWA) announced that Benjamin Lach, The Echo editor, has been awarded a third place in the news category of the 7th Annual Rodeo Press Contest.

Lach received the honor for his news coverage (The Echo, November, 1975 issue) of the 44th Annual Texas Prison Rodeo in Huntsville. He is the first inmate from the Texas Department of Corrections to be recognized in this national competition.

Benjamin Lach

Third — News Category

Levis   I.R.W.A.*

Rodeo Press Contest

*International Rodeo Writers Association

CERTIFICATE OF RECOGNITION

A check for $25, a gift certificate for a pair of Levi's jeans and an award certificate was given to Lach.

Entries in the contest included articles from The New York Times, Dallas Morning News, New Mexico Magazine, Seattle Times and other noted national publications.

Lach has received numerous awards since becoming editor of The Echo. Bud Johns, spokesman for the contest, said, "We hope to see more of your work in our current competition."

The annual contest started in 1970. It is nationally recognized for its effort in honoring writers and photographers for rodeo events. Levi Strauss & Co., in cooperation with the IRWA, sponsor the annual writing contest.

While in prison, Benjamin Lach was editor of *The Echo* newspaper, winning several awards for his writing. (Author collection.)

Are you sorry?

"No. . . . I'm sorry for being in here. I think I've learned a lot and gained a lot of insight in people's actions around me and how I relate to people and how they relate to me and how I exhibit my personality. I feel that it was quite a valuable experience in here."

During the interview, Lach had kind words for the Lubbock newspaper, saying he enjoyed reading the *A-J* in the prison library.

"I used to subscribe for about a year until I ran out of money. . . . The *A-J* covers all the local news, covers a lot of national news and goes into a lot of sports detail. I like the layout style. In fact, my next issue will be a takeoff on the *A-J*. I like the main interest story on top in a box . . . it adds a lot. The language is understandable to the common reader. It's a paper I'd like to work for."

Lach would serve as *Echo* editor from December 1974 through September 1983, writing several award-winning editorials. In some issues during that period of time, not only did Lach publish editorials, but convicted murderers James Cross Jr. and Paul Krueger wrote columns under the heading, "Carte Blanche."

Among the subject titles of Lach's well-written editorials were "Growing of Age," "Roots," "Making It on Furlough," "There Is a Chance for Ex-Offenders," "To Vote or Not to Vote," "Scared Straight Approach," "Men and Rehabilitation," "Are We All in This Together," "Prison Rodeo Perspective," "Music Is Pleasant to the Ear," "Having Cake, Eating It Too," "Head-Running," and "About Prisoners: Myth or Fact?"

As the *Echo* editor, Lach received recognition for his journalistic efforts, including a third-place newswriting award from Levi Strauss & Co. and the International Rodeo Writers Association for his coverage of the 1975 Texas Prison Rodeo. Prizes included a $25 check, a gift certificate for a pair of Levi's jeans, and an award certificate.

Photos from the rodeo depict Lach as a somewhat dashing figure, with a Humphrey Bogart look in western garb. The Texas Prison Rodeo was a tradition born in 1931 and held every Sunday in October in a 30,000-seat arena. During its heyday, the rodeo generated $175,000 in annual revenue.

Acknowledging another skill (craftsman) of Lach's was none other than former Lubbock police detective Floyd "Butch" Hargrave. "I was in Huntsville—Walls Unit—one time and walked into the hobby shop, where Ben [Lach] had made the prettiest mother of pearl belt buckles," Hargrave said.

Jim Willett, who worked in the Texas prison system for thirty years—starting as a guard and working his way up to warden of the Walls Unit—also knew Lach.

"He probably was considered a model prisoner," Willett said in a 2008 interview. "I ran across many an inmate who was [a model prisoner], but could not keep their business straight on the streets. Maybe they needed someone telling them what to do at every turn and to make sure they didn't have easy access to drugs or alcohol. . . . I don't ever recall having a problem with Lach, and I do remember him as being a friendly sort, generally with a smile on his face. My recollection was that he was busy trying to better himself and make things better for other prisoners."

Willett later served as director of the Texas Prison Museum in Huntsville.

In September 1975, several months before Knapp's article appeared, Lach granted an interview to UPI reporter James Overton.

"It's a sensitive job weighing the importance of editorial matters," Lach said of his newspaper duties. "It enables me to express views, opinions and happenings behind the walls. I'm fair to the inmates and everyone else. But I do get negative reports." Lach admitted he did not have free rein in the editorial process. "They don't call it censorship, but all copy has to be approved."

And reflecting on prison life, Lach offered his own perspective.

"The prison as we have it today is a university of crime," he said. "People are negative when they come here. I feel through the publication of *The Echo* it will enhance the attitude of society of what prison life is like. It used to be prisons were a hole in the wall where you dumped people like garbage. But I think society doesn't realize the person who's temporarily out of their hair will be back.

"Eventually you know he's going back outside—why send him back with a negative attitude? Education is the answer—for inmates and society. Rehabilitation is not forced upon you here. It's something you have for your own use."

Although Lach would later tell Knapp he would like to pursue a career in journalism, he related in the UPI interview that he desired to return to college for work on a doctorate in behavioral psychology. (He was elected president of the Psychology Scholarship Society in prison in June 1980.)

"I've been through here and I've seen the life behind bars," Lach said. "My main regret is being here. I might as well make the most of it while I am here. I think I'm still fresh. Every day is a challenge to me. I enjoy going to work each day. As long as you have hope and are optimistic about the future, it keeps you going."

In addition to newspaper interviews, quotes from Lach could be found in at least two books.

Author James R. Hugunin, in the preface of his 1999 book *A Survey of the Representation of Prisoners in the United States: Discipline and Photographs, The Prison Experience*, gives mention of Benjamin Lach in the following excerpt:

As both a discourse and a real place, the penitentiary is the central means by which this social "Other" in our society is—figuratively and literally—tamed and bound. Yet as (Laura) Mulvey's comments suggest, the penitentiary has also been the site of rebellion, of counter-discourses. As Foucault puts it, "no matter how terrifying a given system may be, there always remain the possibilities of resistance, disobedience, and oppositional groupings."

M. Arc, an anthropologist convicted on a security matter, observes in an essay that a duality of behavior—the appearance of conformity to the official system coexisting with an "underground pattern of nonconformity" meant to maintain one's individuality—exists in prisons to this day. Writings from prison, inmate-edited prison journals, poetry and artwork by prisoners constitute instances of such resistance. But there is a pernicious "catch-22" in this, a limit point to resistance. If the prisoner's resistance is viewed by officials and the public alike as mere rebelliousness, it may confirm the public's negative stereotype of the prisoner.

Benjamin Lach, editor of the "Echo" of the Texas state prison in 1980, remarks apropos to this issue that inmates "are viewed as the trash of society, and the only way I have to change that is to continue doing what I am doing every day—namely being a model prisoner." But model prisoners aren't rebellious. How then to achieve empowerment?

Lach is also quoted in James McGrath Morris's 2002 book *Jailhouse Journalism*, which chronicles the history of prison newspapers:

> The *Manual of Correctional Standards* issued by the American Correctional Association in 1966 suggested that "when officials and inmates appreciate each other's position . . . there is little need for strict censorship." More often than not, this prediction came true because the administration sent a clear message to the inmate-editor. "The realistic situation we need to face," said Benjamin Lach, editor of the *Echo* of the Texas state prison in 1980, "is that the administration here has no regard for the inmates, be they editors or non-editors." The only thing he dared to print in the 1980s concerning the administration of the overcrowded and dangerous Texas prison was what came from the front office.

During his incarceration, Lach continued to communicate with Joan Dominick of Lubbock, his friend and alibi witness. The two sent secret messages by shading certain passages in a book of Hebrew poetry they passed back and forth. The book was later confiscated by authorities.

SIDEBAR: ECHOES OF PAROLE

Convicted murderer Bill White preceded Lach as editor of *The Echo* and had his own unique path in arriving behind bars. While employed as a recruiting and information officer for the Texas National Guard in Austin in 1965, White escorted a Camp Mabry personnel clerk to a Christmas party. His date was found strangled in her apartment the morning after the party, and White was convicted of murder with malice and sentenced to life in prison.

White had attended the University of Texas Journalism School and written for *The Daily Texan* student newspaper. He served eight years in prison (*Echo* editor 1967–1974) before being released to become an award-winning sportswriter in Clearwater, Florida.

Inmate Paul Krueger, who contributed several columns to *The Echo*, had an interesting story to tell as well.

As a wayward youth, Krueger, accompanied by a friend and for no apparent reason, shot and killed three innocent fishermen near Corpus Christi, Texas. This was in 1965, and Krueger was seventeen at the time. Although sentenced to life in prison, he furthered his education while being tagged a model prisoner.

While incarcerated, Krueger earned a high school diploma, an associate degree from Lee College, and a bachelor's in psychology with a 4.0 grade-point average through Sam Houston State University. He had also been a construction clerk aide to the prison psychiatrist and assisted in the prison's alcohol-and-drug-abuse programs.

He was so highly regarded that a couple of years prior to his release, this note was attached to his file: "This is probably the most exceptional inmate at TDC. There is nothing further he could do to rehabilitate himself."

Krueger received parole with special consideration in January 1979, serving just thirteen years of a life sentence.

Out of prison, Krueger thrived, continuing on the successful path begun in prison. He earned a master's degree in psychology at California State University at Los Angeles, and a PhD in sociology at South Dakota State University.

He then started a new life as Dr. Paul Krueger, working as a human resources manager and later as a popular business/education professor from 1994 to 2003 at Idaho State, Augustana College, and finally Penn State University. When Krueger's past was discovered by Penn State officials in 2003, however, he resigned under pressure, and his academic future was quickly thrown into limbo.

Eerily similar to the Krueger case was the story of James Wolcott.

On August 5, 1967, the fifteen-year-old shot his mother, father (a college professor), and sister to death in their Georgetown, Texas, home. After confessing to the crime, the youth was found not guilty by reason of insanity. He stayed in Rusk State Hospital for six years, until his release in 1974 at age twenty-one.

Returning to society, Wolcott changed his legal name to James St. James and earned three degrees in psychology at Stephen F. Austin University, Texas Woman's University, and the University of Illinois. He joined the faculty at Millikin University in Decatur, Illinois, in 1986. The award-winning professor and department chairman's past was revealed for the first time in 2013 by a reporter from the *Georgetown Advocate* newspaper. The story went national, sparking considerable controversy.

But unlike Penn State and Paul Krueger, the school stood by Professor St. James, and he continued teaching. Now in his seventies, St. James is professor emeritus at Millikin.

CHAPTER 11

PAROLE BIDS

A LITTLE MORE THAN A MONTH AFTER BENJAMIN Lach's interview with Dave Knapp appeared in the *A-J*, the Texas Board of Pardons and Paroles in Austin rejected his first parole bid. This would mark just the beginning of a long and concentrated effort by some to free the prisoner.

Prior to the decision, Clyde Whiteside, chairman of the parole board, said the inmate had been interviewed by a panel of board members. Whiteside noted that in the weeks leading up to the decision, the board had received a flurry of mail concerning the parole review.

"We have a good bit of correspondence on it [possible parole] in our files," he said, declining to reveal the number of letters received that were "for" or "against" the prisoner's release. The chairman added the letters would have little effect on the decision, saying that the board would follow its regular procedure of considering the severity and gravity of the crime, the effect on the community, etc.

Jay Floyd, administrative assistant to Texas Gov. Dolph Briscoe, said the governor had received "four or five" letters opposing the parole bid.

"If I make a statement, it obviously won't be in favor of parole," said Alton Griffin, who served as special prosecutor in the Lach trial.

"I won't ask a jury to send a man up and then say they gave him too much time."

Added co-prosecutor Cherry: "Lach's a lot smarter than the average inmate—he's smart enough to figure out what to do to please people, and then be able to go out and do it. . . . But he still killed a woman. For the protection of the public and as a deterrent to any potential murderers, I don't think he should be let out after this short a time."

But Lach had his supporters, too, as letters were sent on his behalf by the Bialystoker Home and Infirmary for the Aged in New York and appeals attorney Joe Shaffer. The Bialystoker Home was an organization founded by Bialystoker immigrants with headquarters in New York City. The mission of the organization was to maintain an active, compassionate concern for the well-being of those immigrants (Lach was born in Bialystok, Poland).

Trial judge Byron Matthews even spoke out, at least, almost: "[My] philosophy is that a jury speaks for itself. But in this particular case, I might make a comment when the time comes. When and if I do . . ."

Many years later, Beverly Barnes, a granddaughter of victim Alice Morgan, provided a more direct assessment. "We hated the fact that he wasn't actually suffering in prison, but instead in charge of the local prison newspaper and working on getting his [college] degree," she said in a 2014 interview. "He deserved death, just like he'd given her."

One year later, on May 23, 1977, the parole board once again rejected Lach's parole attempt. Board Chairman Paul F. Cromwell said that in making its decision, the board considered the nature of the offense and believed the thirty-two-year-old Lach had an assaultive personality.

Alton Griffin, by then Lubbock County criminal district attorney (a new position that combined the county attorney and district attorney offices) told the board that he believed Lach was "dangerous to society. Every time he comes up, I'll be here," Griffin said.

Lach's mother Lucy and his brother, along with members of the Polish American community in Boston, also appeared before the board in Austin.

Cromwell said the board had received "sixteen or seventeen" protest letters against the parole, mostly from interested persons in the Lubbock area.

A third parole hearing was on the horizon in 1979. John T. Montford, who had replaced Griffin as Lubbock criminal district attorney, said he had received a report that critical portions of Lach's psychiatric file may have been missing from state penitentiary records. Montford told the *A-J* he planned to travel to Austin within two weeks to attempt to verify the report with the parole board.

After receiving the report of the missing file, Montford called Lach's prison psychiatrist to check the accuracy of the report. The doctor responded, "Where did you get that?" but neither confirmed nor denied the report.

The psychiatrist told the *A-J* he was "not at liberty to discuss TDC [Texas Department of Corrections] matters with newspapers" and referred the inquiry to penitentiary system attorney Bob DeLong. DeLong said he had conducted his own inquiry and determined "there is no missing file."

Connie L. Jackson, board chair, confirmed that Lach was being seriously considered for parole. She had personally interviewed Lach in Huntsville recently and revealed that the three-member board would review the case in May or June 1979. "We're still in the process of studying all the available information and facts," she said.

Meanwhile, Blair Cherry left no doubt where he stood on the pending decision. "I would guess that there's not two or three more people in the world who know more about [Lach] than I do," Cherry told the *A-J*.

Cherry said he and Griffin sought the death penalty for Lach because they were afraid that he would eventually be paroled. "We made the decision because we felt so strongly that if he ever did get out of prison, he would be a danger to society," Cherry said. "With the parole system working the way it does, we knew it would be a very short time before he would be eligible for parole."

Cherry said it was no surprise that Lach was a model prisoner.

"In our discussions with the doctors that had him at Rusk State Hospital, they predicted that if he went to prison, he would make a model prisoner, which I understand he has. But they also stressed that if he ever got out of a structured environment like a prison or a hospital, they were very concerned that he would be tempted to resort to violence if he were threatened or he thought it was necessary."

Added Cherry: "The consensus of all the psychiatrists and psychologists connected with him during the entire period of time that we were handling him was that he was an anti-social or sociopathic person. He is the type of individual who, if he ever got caught in a similar situation, would be very likely to do what he did again."

Cherry acknowledged that he was sympathetic to Lach and his family, as they tried to survive as Jews in Poland and Israel before immigrating to the United States. He stated, "I feel sorry for [Lach]. There's a lot of Benjamin's background that would tend to make you feel sorry for him. However, the job of the criminal justice system is to protect society from persons who cannot live within the rules, and I think that virtually everyone connected with the case thinks he would be a danger to society if he were set free. I'm sure there's some caseworker down there with the Board of Pardons and Paroles that thinks he's the brightest guy there is. And he probably is. But the Board of Pardons and Paroles must take under consideration that he would be a danger to society if he were paroled. I feel pretty strongly about it. Feeling sorry for him and turning him loose are two different things. He needs to be restrained, in my opinion."

The board rejected Lach's request for parole on June 4, 1979. Prior to the hearing, Montford wrote a letter of protest, and Alton Griffin traveled to Austin in May to argue against the parole. After denying the request, the board said Lach's case would again come up for review in 1980.

The convicted murderer's name soon made national headlines when, on June 13, 1979, it was reported that Benjamin Lach received a certificate naming him as one of the "1979 Outstanding Young Men of

America" for his work as a Huntsville Jaycee. The certificate was given "in recognition of outstanding professional achievement, superior leadership ability, and exceptional service to the community."

Jim Michaels, a spokesman for the national Jaycees organization, said the award was not given by the national group and not related to the "10 Outstanding Young Men of America" program that the Jaycees conducted each year. However, Michaels said the awards and "Who's Who" type of book are published and distributed by a "national advisory board" and endorsed by the national Jaycees. "The [program] is a very good program and the [awards book] has 936 pages of names in very small print," Michaels said.

He said any Jaycee may be nominated for inclusion by a chapter or an individual. "It is strictly a non-U.S. Jaycees event, even though we endorse it," he said.

Texas Jaycees would later protest the award at a national convention, and the national organization withdrew its endorsement of the awards directory.

Lach's next parole attempt came before the board in May 1980. This time, the two parole board commissioners assigned to review Lach's case split their vote one-to-one on whether to grant parole. Under Texas law, this meant that another board member (Chairman Connie Jackson) would be required to review the case and determine whether it should be forwarded to the governor, who would ultimately make the final decision.

Once again, Montford weighed in on the matter, sending a four-page letter of protest to the board and Gov. William P. Clements.

Montford cited forty-one pages of transcribed testimony from psychological experts who, twelve years earlier, predicted Lach would be a model prisoner; parole was again denied.

Although Lach was still imprisoned in July 1982, officials from the Lubbock County Criminal District Attorney's Office were understandably upset when they discovered Lach had been granted two furloughs during the previous eleven months to visit friends in Houston.

"I really can't give you information on them [furloughs] other than yes, he got a couple of furloughs," Texas Department of Corrections spokesman Jay Byrd told the *A-J*. "He did not, evidently, get into any trouble."

Said Don McBeath, spokesman for the Lubbock County Criminal DA's Office: "Mr. [John] Montford and myself and some other people in this office are disturbed by that [furloughs]. . . . Psychiatrists testified at the trial that Lach, placed in a proper environment at the proper time could kill again. As long as he's in a controlled, disciplined environment, you can alleviate that. When you release him for a few days on an apparent vacation, you are no longer able to control, confine or discipline him. . . . We know that with good time, he will be out of prison in a few years. There's nothing we can do to prevent that. That's the way the system works. But I don't think he should be out until that time comes."

McBeath said the county district attorney would send a letter protesting the furloughs to the TDC.

Byrd, the TDC spokesman, said the criteria for granting furloughs "varies from inmate to inmate—the amount of time he has done on his sentence, what kind of record he's maintained while he's in prison, whether or not he's had any escapes before." He added that most furloughs are for three to five days, and that Lach was last out of prison "several months ago." Byrd said that inmates apply for furloughs, and their applications are considered first by their warden and then by a committee comprised of officials in the inmate classification division.

"Where they go and what they do is classification's confidential information," Byrd said. "It's also approved by the county they go to. We inform the county sheriff, and he had to approve it."

Lach's furloughs were in September 1981 and March 1982.

"He left at the appropriate time and returned prior to the appropriate time," said Huntsville Unit Warden Jack Pursley. "It's a privilege that all of our inmates that have good conduct and good work records and have satisfied the rules and regulations that we govern under are eligible to be considered for. In his case, he has maintained a good record in TDC, and he was eligible for consideration and he did get a furlough."

Pursley pointed out that Lach "is getting pretty short on his sentence," with a scheduled discharge date, if not paroled before then, of August 7, 1988.

Lach's seventh parole hearing was scheduled for May 1983.

As in previous years, former Lubbock County Criminal District Attorney and by then State Sen. John T. Montford aggressively fought the parole. In an April 1983 interview with the *A-J*, Montford said he had heard that there was growing support within the TDC and the parole board for Lach's release.

"There have been some rumblings going around and I think they're going to make another run," Montford said. "He just does a snow job on them. I think he's one of the most dangerous criminals of our time."

Montford said that he would again be sending a letter of protest, along with other pertinent information to the parole board and Gov. Mark White.

"[Lach's] a model prisoner, editor of the (TDC inmates') paper," Montford said. "We need to keep him as a model prisoner and not let him on the streets."

Earlier, State Sen. Kent Caperton of Bryan said he had been asked to intervene on behalf of Lach. An aide to Caperton, whose district included Huntsville, said the senator was contacted by some constituents the previous year after Lach was denied parole.

"He has an outstanding record since he has been incarcerated and has accomplished some amazing things," the Caperton aide said of Lach. "But upon looking into the matter, we found out about the severity of the crime. That has had a lot to do with his parole being denied. It looks like, with the severity of the crime, that he might have to go to mandatory parole." The aide noted that Caperton took no position in the case after he inquired about Lach to both the parole board and to Montford.

For the seventh time, parole was denied, with the three parole commissioners voting two-to-one against. If Lach had received a two-to-one vote in his favor, the decision on parole would have gone to the governor for a final decision.

Parole commissioner Ron Jackson voted for the parole, while commissioners Glenn Heckmann and Sue Cunningham voted against.

Parole Board Executive Director John Byrd said the reasons cited by the commissioners voting against the parole were "the nature and seriousness of the offense and that it was assaultive."

This marked the third year in a row Lach had received one favorable vote. In the previous two years, a parole board member had to break the tie. The parole process changed the previous year to give three of the nine parole commissioners all three votes, with the votes arriving in a package at the Austin parole board headquarters.

In separate interviews in 2005, Alton Griffin and Blair Cherry offered their thoughts on the parole process.

"He [Benjamin Lach] was the only person I ever protested when they came up for parole," Griffin said. "Of all the people I ever tried, I thought he was probably the most likely to commit another offense. I felt that he was most dangerous and just couldn't shake that compulsion to please his mother."

"The real struggle was keeping him in prison until his mandatory release date," Cherry said. "He first came up for parole in the 1970s, and I opposed his release on parole at that time."

SIDEBAR: THE HUNTSVILLE PRISON SIEGE

The Walls Unit captured national attention during the 1974 Huntsville Prison Siege. On July 24, 1974, inmate Fred Carrasco and two fellow inmates held eleven prison employees hostage in the prison library. Ten days and several demands later, Carrasco and company attempted a daring escape using the hostages as shields. During the ensuing shootout, two female hostages were shot to death by their captors, one of the three prisoners was shot to death by authorities, and Carrasco committed suicide.

While all this drama was taking place, Lach was incarcerated in the Eastham Unit in Lovelady, Texas, twenty-seven miles north of

Huntsville. He moved to the Huntsville Walls Unit in December 1974 to serve as editor of *The Echo*.

CHAPTER 12

THE EDUCATION
OF A FREE MAN

THE BUSINESS OF THE BOARD OF PARDONS AND
Paroles in Texas has certainly seen its share of controversy through the
years. The prison population doubled in the span of a decade, from
15,000 inmates in 1972 to 30,000 in 1981. Various court rulings, changing laws and procedures, political influence, and public pressure all contribute to making the process difficult to fully comprehend.

Add to the mix legislation with special provisions that enable inmates
to receive good time credit for earning college degrees and ultimately
early release from prison and you have, well, more confusion.

Such was the case on October 31, 1983, as detailed on the front page
of the *Lubbock Evening Avalanche-Journal*:

> Lach Freed: New Law Speeds Slayer's Release
> By Bob Campbell, Evening Journal Staff
> Benjamin Lach, whose scalpel slaying of a Texas Tech University
> woman custodian 16 years ago became perhaps the most infamous

murder case in Lubbock history, has been released from the Texas Department of Corrections under guidelines of a Texas Senate bill.

Lach was given extra "good time" credit under Senate Bill 640 passed this year and has been released on final discharge from the TDC. A TDC spokesman this morning said Lach was released last Friday after prison officials determined that he had enough educational credits, under Arlington Sen. Bob McFarland's Senate bill, to discharge the rest of his 40-year sentence.

"I talked with him, and I think he was going back to his parents in Massachusetts," TDC spokesman Charles Brown said. "It was just a pretty straight-out discharge."

Under previous regulations, Lach's discharge date was not due to arrive until August 1988. He had been denied parole each spring since he became eligible in the mid-1970s, most recently last spring when one of three parole commissioners voted for his release.

Lach had been released on several "furloughs" in the past two years to see family members in Houston, and McFarland indicated this morning that those releases probably were considered evidence of the 38-year-old inmate's trustworthiness.

McFarland said the bill, which went into effect June 17, came out of the prison reform commission appointed by former Gov. William P. Clements. "What's happened here is the department has just now finalized the criteria for good time credit for trusty positions," McFarland said. "That's being applied to inmates now."

The bill allowed additional good time credit for the top two classifications of trusties, which included Lach.

State Sen. John T. Montford was in trial this morning and unavailable for comment. But he always has strongly opposed parole of Lach.

Former Lubbock Criminal District Attorney Alton Griffin, special prosecutor in the Lach case in 1970 after Lach was released from the Rusk State Hospital for the Criminally Insane, was surprised that Lach could gain enough extra credit to gain release, in effect, almost five years early. "I wasn't aware of anything that would

After serving a little more than fifteen years of his forty-year sentence, with an exemplary prison record, Benjamin Lach was released from prison in 1983. (*Lubbock Avalanche-Journal* morgue file collection, the Southwest Collection.)

give him the opportunity to get any more good time to obtain a discharge this early," Griffin said. "I went over what the discharge date would be with the people in the parole office a number of years ago, and 1988 was always the discharge date."

Referring to what he said has been a pro-Lach faction within the TDC to gain his release, Griffin said, "Very obviously, there have been some people trying."

Criminal District Attorney Jim Bob Darnell said he was upset that he was not notified of Lach's release until learning about it indirectly today. "I didn't expect Lach's name to be brought up again until next spring," Darnell said. "I was a little bit shocked, to say the least." Darnell said he will write a letter to the TDC to protest their failure to notify him.

Lach's parents live in Brookline, Mass., the TDC spokesman said.

He was apprehended in the spring of 1968 by city detectives, who chased him from a professor's office that was being broken into.

The slain woman, Sarah Alice Morgan, was found almost decapitated by a science laboratory scalpel in December 1967 in a campus science building laboratory.

Lach was editor of the TDC inmate newspaper for several years and reportedly was a personal favorite of numerous TDC officials.

The early release was met with disapproval by at least some jurors from the Lach trial.

"I don't think that's very good at all; I don't like that at all," said Danny L. Reed of Fort Worth, the jury foreman.

Another juror, J. J. Bilardi, said he had resolved in his mind that Lach would probably be released early anyway, but said the original sentence was not commensurate with the crime. He said he was "definitely not real happy" to see Lach released early because of the new law.

"One thing we didn't understand was what the number of years related to," Bilardi said. "The formulas [for early release] were never explained to us." He added he felt the sentence assessed would have been longer if the jury had known how short a time Lach would actually be imprisoned.

Two other jurors offered similar opinions.

"That's our justice," said James J. Huff. "We didn't know that [about the bill] back then."

Added Mary Shubert: "I thought he was supposed to serve the whole time."

Senate Bill 640 contained four sentences that led to Lach's early release. That portion of the bill allows inmates to accrue good conduct time of up to fifteen days for every thirty days actually served for participation in educational programs. Prior to his imprisonment, Lach earned a bachelor of arts degree in chemistry from Suffolk University (Massachusetts), in 1967. During his incarceration, he obtained an associate degree in business administration from Lee College in 1975; a bachelor of science degree in psychology from Sam Houston State University in 1978; an associate degree in psychology from Lee College in 1982; and a bachelor of business administration from Sam Houston State University in 1982. Lee College, based in Baytown, Texas, is a junior college that offered courses at the Huntsville prison.

The bill awarded Lach three additional years of credit, which Senator McFarland said translated into twelve to fifteen months of actual time, with good conduct time taken into consideration. "So, he would have been out in 12 to 15 months even without the education credit," McFarland said.

Lach actually served fifteen years, seven months, and seventeen days of his forty-year sentence. This included his time in the Lubbock County Jail, Rusk State Hospital, and prison.

TDC spokesman Rick Hartley explained that the prison system used a two-step calculation in determining the release. Under the first calculation, using his good conduct time credits for being a trusty (a prisoner who has earned the trust of prison authorities for model behavior), Lach would have received a discharge date of March 1984. In the second calculation, as a result of the law's educational provisions, Lach was scheduled for release on October 28, 1983.

"His discharge was fully under the policy provided in the law and there was nothing unusual about it," Hartley said. "We had no authority to hold him further."

In a follow-up article in the *A-J* on November 1, staff writer Bob Campbell wrote:

BENJAMIN LACH, convicted 13 years ago of one of the most sensational murders in Lubbock's history, was in his home state of Massachusetts Monday, a free and unrestricted man because of an obscure piece of legislation that mandated his release from the state prison in Huntsville.

The article continued:

A Texas Senate bill passed unanimously earlier this year advanced Lach's mandatory discharge date by almost four years. He was released in Huntsville on Friday and was back home in Brookline, Mass., by Monday.

Under the bill, which Sen. John T. Montford and 29 other state senators voted for, Lach was given "good time" credit for educational advancement—the two bachelor's and two associate degrees he had earned since his 1970 imprisonment for the 1967 murder of Sarah Alice Morgan, a Texas Tech woman custodian.

Before the bill, sponsored by Sen. Bob McFarland of Arlington, was approved in a 30–0 vote, Lach was not scheduled to be released, barring parole, until August 7, 1988. He was denied parole in his most recent hearing held earlier this year.

"All we're doing is complying with the law," said TDC spokesman Charles Brown. "We didn't let Ben Lach out because we wanted to let him out. He just had enough time accrued."

Montford, who was Lubbock County's criminal district attorney prior to his election to the Senate, was in court participating in a civil case all day Monday and could not be reached for comment.

"There was considerable discussion," McFarland told the *Avalanche-Journal*. "I recall very little, if any, opposition in the House or Senate. It was supported by all the state agencies and the TDC."

"There is always going to be an instance of earlier release where someone feels that the crime didn't justify that release," the senator said. "Yet the sentencing entity set a 40-year sentence for what I recollect was a fairly heinous offense."

"It means somebody is going to get out earlier than they would have had the legislature not established these incentives, and somebody is going to get out who was involved in a very controversial crime," McFarland said.

Lach's elderly father, Herman Lach, said Monday afternoon his son was at the library in Brookline and will stay in the Massachusetts town while deciding where to apply for work.

In a tense, somewhat excited voice Lach answered the phone later in the day, acknowledged twice that he was Benjamin Lach, but then hung up when told the caller was a newspaper reporter in Lubbock.

After the release, John Byrd, executive director of the Pardons and Parole Board, reflected on Lach's failed parole efforts.

"We would just get bombarded with correspondence from Lubbock," he said. "It was very much on the minds of the Lubbock community. . . . He was one of the few Jewish inmates in TDC and had very strong backing from the Jewish community in Houston."

Regardless, Lach received his release at a "good" time. Amidst federal lawsuits and ensuing prison reform handed down by Judge William Wayne Justice, longtime Texas Department of Corrections Director W. J. "James" Estelle Jr. resigned—the same month Lach was released. During the next two years (1984–1985), escalating gang violence resulted in fifty-two inmates murdered and 700 more stabbed in Texas prisons. That was more violence than had been seen the entire previous decade.

SIDEBAR: JAMES CROSS, KENNETH MCDUFF, AND THE PAROLE SYSTEM

In 1992, nine years after Benjamin Lach's discharge from prison, convicted murderer James Cross Jr. received a similar release with a similar reaction.

Cross, an Army veteran and twenty-two-year-old sophomore English major at the University of Texas, was arrested in 1965 for the murder of UT coeds Susan Rigsby and Shirley Stark of Dallas.

Cross had once dated Stark, a fellow student in a UT biology class. The two sorority sisters disappeared on July 18, and twelve days later, their bodies were found in a field north of Austin. Both had been strangled. Cross confessed to killing the women in his Austin apartment and later dumping the bodies. The brutal crime sent shockwaves throughout Austin and the state.

According to his confession, Cross said at that about 1 p.m. on July 18, 1965, Stark called and asked if she and Rigsby could come by his apartment to clean up and change clothes. Rigsby showered at the apartment, but when she walked from the bathroom into the bedroom, Cross grabbed her and choked her until she collapsed on the bed. When Stark came out of the bathroom, Cross did the same until she fell to the floor. Hearing a semi-conscious Rigsby moaning on the bed, Cross raped her, then choked her to death. He told police that he killed Stark to quiet her when the woman sat upright and began to scream. Later that night, with the bodies still in his apartment, Cross went on a date. About 3 a.m., he loaded the bodies in Stark's Corvair and dumped them in a field.

Cross was convicted of the Rigsby murder in 1966, with the prosecution asking for the death penalty; instead, the jury brought back a life sentence. Cross won a second trial in 1986 following a US Supreme Court ruling applied retroactively concerning how it is determined whether a defendant is competent to stand trial. While awaiting retrial in 1987, Cross posted bond and gained freedom for six weeks. During that time, he married a woman who had interviewed him in prison three years earlier.

The prosecution couldn't seek the death penalty again since a jury had previously sentenced him to life. During the retrial, jurors heard testimony that Cross had killed the women because of sadistic sexual fantasies and sentenced him to eighty years in prison. He could not be tried for the murder of Stark because in the 1970s his lawyers had submitted a motion demanding a speedy trial and the state decided to dismiss the case.

Like Lach, Cross was described by all as a model prisoner. At the retrial in 1987, four prison officials and psychiatrists/psychologists testified that he would not be a threat to society if released.

While incarcerated, Cross earned bachelor's degrees in humanities, general studies, and behavioral science from the University of Houston–Clear Lake. He obtained a master's degree in humanities from the same university and an associate degree in arts from Alvin Community College.

Much like Benjamin Lach, Cross came up for parole many times (twenty) but was denied each time.

But on September 30, 1992, fifty-year-old James C. Cross Jr., after serving twenty-seven years, walked out of the Huntsville prison a free man (with no supervision), thanks to the state's "good-time" policy (credit earned for good behavior and educational achievement) that reduced his sentence by fifty-three years.

And Cross, like Benjamin Lach, was not paroled but fully released, meaning that neither would be under supervision from the authorities. Had they been paroled, they would have been supervised by a parole officer for a number of years.

"I like Jim Cross," his attorney David Botsford told the *Austin American-Statesman* in 1992. "He's very intelligent, a very sensitive human being. He feels very deeply that what he did was wrong and that he needed to be punished, which is why, in part, he gave his confession to [Austin Police] Chief (George) Phifer.... The Jim Cross of 1987 was not the same Jim Cross of 1965.... He would like to get out and become a productive member of society."

Looking back, Phifer said he was unsure whether authorities would have been able to gather enough evidence to bring Cross to trial without the confession.

Recalling his first encounter with Cross, Phifer said in an interview with the *Statesman*: "He was an intelligent young fellow, but he had a facial expression that caused you to doubt. [It was] something in his eyes. The way his eyes looked. Once you got past that, you could tell he was a pleasant person, an intelligent person. . . . I didn't see him as a monster although he did a monstrous thing. These things are sometimes beyond comprehension as to why things happen. Whether James Cross was remorseful in his heart, only James Cross will know."

Cross declined media interviews on the day of his discharge, but his attorney read a brief statement in which he promised Cross would be a productive member of society and would pose no threat to the public.

After his release, Cross left the Walls Unit, jumped into the backseat of his attorney's car, and put his arm around his wife Gloria, a former Dallas probation officer. The car then sped away.

That same day, the Coalition for a Safer Society, an umbrella organization of crime victims' rights groups, held a press conference at the Texas State Capitol to urge the Texas Legislature to change the "good time" policies.

"Where is justice? Where is common sense?" asked coalition member Matt Harnest. "The punishment needs to fit the crime. . . . I think the jurors weren't aware that when they gave him 80 years that he'd be out in 27."

A postscript from Cross's attorney Botsford in 2022: "Jim periodically kept in touch with me after his release and to my knowledge, never violated the law after his release. He died a number of years later [in 2001 at age fifty-nine], and my memory is that he had congested arteries from consuming prison food for more than 27 years." He continued, "Some people commit horrible crimes—situational to be sure—but are nevertheless capable of rehabilitation/redemption."

Through the years, early release/parole continued to be a controversial subject in Texas. In 1966, authorities arrested Kenneth McDuff for the rape and murder of three Texas teenagers in what came to be known as the "Broomstick murders." McDuff received the death penalty but had his sentence overturned in 1972 when the US Supreme Court abolished capital punishment.

McDuff was supposed to serve a life sentence but, due in part to overcrowded prisons, received parole on a two-to-one vote in September 1989. One observer would later state that the 1989 parole of McDuff was the "biggest mistake ever by the Texas parole board."

A year later, McDuff saw his parole revoked after making a terroristic threat to a high school student. But after only two months back in prison, McDuff was once again granted parole. From 1989 to 1992, he would go on a murder spree and become one of America's most notorious serial killers (although some of his many confessions were questionable). Eventually, he was recaptured, and after public outrage over his previous releases, administered the death penalty on November 17, 1998.

After McDuff's second arrest for murder in 1992, Texas launched a massive overhaul of its prison system in an effort to prevent violent criminals from winning early parole. The tightened parole rules, extensive prison building construction projects, and upgraded monitoring of violent parolees became known as the "McDuff Laws."

For example, the tightened rules meant that after September 1, 1993, if a defendant received a life sentence for capital murder, he/she must serve a minimum of forty calendar years before even being considered for parole.

Ironically, the deciding vote in McDuff's 1989 parole was cast by parole board member James Granberry, an orthodontist by trade, a former Lubbock mayor, and the 1974 Texas Republican gubernatorial nominee. Appointed to the parole board by Gov. Bill Clements in 1989, Granberry resigned from the board two years later. He then worked as a consultant to represent prisoners before the board he had formerly chaired.

In August 1994, Granberry received a five-year probated sentence from a federal court for perjury, admitting he had given false testimony to a federal magistrate concerning the number of prisoners he had represented after leaving the parole board.

The court ordered Granberry to perform 150 hours of community service and reside in a halfway house for six months.

In 1967, at the time of Alice Morgan's murder, James Granberry was a rising young political star, serving on the Lubbock City Council. Later, as mayor, his leadership helped the city recover from a devastating tornado in 1970.

EPILOGUE

IN THE PAST HALF-CENTURY, THE CITY OF
Lubbock and Texas Tech have experienced impressive growth. In 1967,
the population of Lubbock stood at 164,500; today, it is a bustling community of 257,000 residents, the eleventh-largest city in Texas.

Lubbock is a major retail trading center for a twenty-six-county area
in West Texas, nicknamed the "Hub City" as the economic, education,
and healthcare hub of a region commonly called the South Plains. This
area is the largest contiguous cotton-growing region in the world.

Despite its growth, Lubbock has maintained its national image as a
standard-bearer of conservatism.

In 2005, a national poll ranked Lubbock as the second-most conservative city in the entire country, behind Provo, Utah. Ten years later, a
similar poll did not rank Lubbock because it did not meet the minimum
population requirement.

In 1989, President George Bush responded to accusations that the
US economy was slumping with this quip: "All the people in Lubbock
think things are going great."

Lubbock is commonly known as "the city with a church on every
street corner."

Musicians with Lubbock or Texas Tech ties have kept the memory of
Buddy Holly alive with chart-topping music. Lubbock native Mac Davis

and former Texas Tech architecture student Henry John Deutschendorf
Jr.—better known as John Denver—were fixtures in the country-pop
genre in the 1970s–1980s. Denver was a Grammy-winning pop super-
star, recording such classics as "Rocky Mountain High" and "Take Me
Home, Country Roads."

Both Davis and Denver also acted, appearing in numerous motion
pictures and television shows.

In the mid-1990s, along came the Dixie Chicks, with Lubbock's
Natalie Maines as lead singer. The group had several hit country singles, winning a dozen Grammy Awards and distinguishing themselves
as the best-selling all-female band and best-selling country group in the
US during the Nielsen SoundScan era (1991–present). The group suffered backlash after Maines made a negative comment about President
George W. Bush during a concert, but the band has regained its popu-
larity. In an effort to be more politically correct, the group is now known
as simply The Chicks.

Like the city, Texas Tech has continued to thrive. In terms of enrollment, 18,646 students attended Tech in 1967, and that number had
increased to 40,528 in the fall of 2022.

After many prosperous years as a college, the students and faculty
believed that the name "Texas Technological College" no longer represented the mission of an institution with undergraduates and graduates
in diverse subjects. A number of name changes were proposed, including
that of "Texas State University," which was preferred by a large number
of students and faculty. However, alumni and the board of directors,
wanting to ensure that the "Double T" symbol would remain the school
emblem, favored the name "Texas Tech University."

The name change was such a controversial issue that students
held rallies and even marched against the proposed name Texas Tech
University. Despite the protests and several votes by students and faculty
members to change the name of Texas Technological College to Texas
State University, the board did not waver. During a ten-year period of
controversy, many other names surfaced, including the University of

The Science Building today, home to classrooms, labs, and offices in the departments of geosciences and physics. (Texas Tech University Press photo.)

West Texas, the Texas State University of Arts, Sciences and Technology, Texas Technological University, Texas Technological College and State University, and the University of the Southwest. Finally, in 1969, the board voted unanimously to change the name to Texas Tech University. Texas governor Preston Smith signed a bill into law making the name change official.

The campus has undergone extensive changes as well, with a number of additions and improvements to both its academic programs and physical facilities. The university now consists of thirteen colleges offering 150 undergraduate programs, 100 graduate degrees, and fifty doctoral programs.

The Texas Tech University Health Sciences Center was created by the Texas Legislature in 1969 as a separate educational institution to address problems of healthcare delivery in rural areas and to develop education programs emphasizing primary care throughout West Texas. Recently added to the portfolio was a veterinary school located in Amarillo.

The office (324) shown in the early 2000s that, in 1967, was Professor Kent Rylander's office in which two Lubbock detectives spent the night as part of a stakeout. (Author photo.)

The biology department, once housed in the Science Building, has its own building, which opened in 1968. The Science Building is home to the physics and geosciences departments, which are identified by signage

Current view of the north wing hallway on the third floor of the Science Building. The last office on the left is Room 331, believed to be the former location of Room 304-J, where the murder of Sarah Alice Morgan occurred. (Courtesy Dr. Walter Borst.)

on the exterior of the building. Located on either side of this edifice are the Chemistry Building and the Mathematics & Statistics Building (in 1967, the Social Science Building was at this location). Boston Avenue runs parallel to the east (front) of the Science Building.

In the fall of 2022, the Texas Tech Board of Regents approved a $16.1 million renovation project for the seventy-year-old Science Building. This will upgrade the HVAC system, provide exterior cosmetic repairs, replace flooring, and upgrade building accessibility and fire alarm and sprinkler systems.

In the years since the murder of Sarah Alice Morgan on the third floor of the Science Building in 1967, many offices and room numbers have been altered. The third floor now houses faculty/graduate student offices from the geosciences department in the north attic (where the murder occurred).

At the time of the Morgan murder in 1967, Room 304-J was a lab, but today is believed to be Room 331, a graduate student office. (Texas Tech University Press photo.)

Offices identified by number in the north attic include 317, 319A (old number of 304B still visible at top of door), 319B (old 304C still visible), 3MB, 321, 323, 325, 327, 330, 331, and 332. There is no office numbered 304-J, the lab in which the murder occurred in 1967. The old 304-J is most likely now in the area near Room 331, which serves as a graduate student office.

Other offices identified by number on the floor are 314, 316, 318, 324, and 332. Room 324 is where police detectives staked out Professor Kent Rylander's office overnight.

In the south wing of the attic are cubicle-like offices for graduate student teaching assistants, numbered 301–306.

Among the many newer facilities on campus are the Jerry Rawls College of Business, English/Philosophy Building, state-of-the-art residence halls, United Supermarkets Arena, Frazier Alumni Pavilion, Kent Hance Chapel, and, as a sign of the times, parking garages. Several athletic facility improvements have been completed, including a modern basketball complex (United Supermarkets Arena), while Jones AT&T Stadium is the beneficiary of numerous ongoing upgrades and expansions.

Also of note is the demolition of the storied old Lubbock Municipal Coliseum in 2019, the site of so many Red Raiders basketball games and frantic class registration experiences.

Rusk State Hospital, where Benjamin Lach was sent for treatment in 1968, is in its second century of operation, having observed its centennial year in 2019. The facility underwent the beginning of a $200 million facelift in 2021, as six buildings were demolished and a new administration building was erected, with a hundred new maximum and non-maximum security beds in the works. The hospital treats approximately 300 patients.

Rusk is an in-patient hospital providing psychiatric treatment and care. It offers adult psychiatric services, maximum security forensic psychiatric services for adult men, forensic competency restoration services, and residential psychiatric services.

Although Rusk's maximum security unit still houses some violent mentally ill offenders, the majority of those individuals are treated at North Texas State Hospital in Vernon, located near Wichita Falls and just six miles south of the Oklahoma-Texas border.

A sign marks the entrance to the City of Lubbock Cemetery, located in the east part of town. The cemetery, established in 1892, is the third largest in Texas. Sarah Alice Morgan and her husband were laid to rest here. (Author collection.)

The City of Lubbock Cemetery is not the easiest place in town to find. Exiting Martin Luther King Boulevard (formerly Quirt Avenue), you pass Dunbar College Preparatory Academy (formerly known as Dunbar Middle School), encounter older east Lubbock neighborhoods, and, in the distance, spot ancient grain yards and elevators. One finally spies the plain, but well-manicured, cemetery grounds off 31st Street.

As difficult as it is to locate the cemetery, it's just as easy to find the grave of Lubbock's most famous citizen—rock and roll pioneer Buddy Holly. Near the entrance to the cedar tree–lined cemetery is a Buddy Holly historical marker, and just a few yards down to the right, just off the road, is the Holly family gravesite. (A small yard sign identifies the Holly grave.)

Another well-known singer-songwriter from Lubbock, Mac Davis, is buried in the cemetery, having died in 2020. That fulfilled the wish of the last lyric—*And when I die you can bury me in Lubbock Texas in my jeans*—of his song "Texas in My Rearview Mirror."

It's a gray, drizzly summer day, and the mosquitoes are out in full force. Another gravesite is not as easy to spot. When a visitor asks a cemetery worker, she politely looks up the name and provides directions. A short drive later and the destination is found—there, perhaps a hundred yards from Buddy Holly's grave, is the gravesite of Sarah Alice Morgan.

A few miles east of the main Tech campus and the downtown area, past Mackenzie Park, is an empty lot (2902 E. 4th Street) where the Morgans' house stood in 1967. The small, white-frame structure was demolished a few years ago in the old, decaying area of town. Just down the street is the Hope Deliverance Temple Church.

The historic North Overton neighborhood was one of the first residential areas in Lubbock. But by the 1980s, the area had declined as old, deteriorating houses and apartments became low-rent eyesores. It got to the point that the high crime area became known as the "Tech Ghetto."

In 1999, local private developer Delbert McDougal, defying the naysayers, spearheaded the Overton Project, beginning with the demolition of old rental houses and apartments, and resulting in the construction of a new hotel and modern student housing, retail outlets, and restaurants.

The modern high-rise Overton Hotel was built in 2009 and located on Mac Davis Lane—Davis grew up just a few blocks away, living in the College Courts Motel at 5th and University. His father owned and operated the business in the 1950s, and it was located directly across the street from Jones Stadium.

Just five blocks south of the Overton Hotel is the site of the F. B. Kyle boardinghouse at 2318 Main Street where Benjamin Lach resided at the time of the 1967 murder of Alice Morgan.

As late as 2003, the house still stood, alone and empty, near an area that had been cleared for the North Overton revitalization effort.

The Kyles' small Spanish-style house (1,700 square feet), built in 1928 and located just a couple of blocks east of the Tech campus (within walking distance), was relatively intact in the early 2000s, sitting eerily abandoned while clusters of new apartments, townhomes, and businesses loomed nearby. Weeds and trees on the lot on the brick street were over-grown, but the square-shaped house itself sported a covered porch and carport to the side.

Since that time, however, the house has been demolished and on its site is a parking lot for St. Elizabeth's Catholic Church. Across the street is an apartment complex and nearby, a block to the west at Main and Avenue X, there once stood a small, old building (built in 1950) that housed Bob's Café in 1967. By the 1970s, the structure at 2401 Main Street was the site of a well-known popular disco nightspot frequented by Tech students known as "Uncle Nasty's." After going through several reincarnations as a club, it was demolished in 2021 as part of the ongoing renovation and is now an empty lot.

As of this writing, fifty-five years have passed since the murder of Sarah Alice Morgan. Today's students and faculty members at Texas Tech are unlikely to be familiar with this bizarre and tragic story. But according to Dr. Kenneth Davis, professor emeritus of English at Tech until his death in 2019, and who was on the faculty in 1967, the murder has taken on an almost ghost-like or folk-like aura.

Not long after the murder, according to lore, the slain woman's image began to appear in the hallway of the Science Building during midterm and final examination times.

"She appeared and, supposedly, she would look at the students through the glass in the door and shake her head sadly," Davis said. "She appears out in the hall looking into the classrooms, and she projects pity as if she were sympathetic to the students' trials at having to work so hard to pass the examinations. The shutters to the doors in most rooms in that building are about half wire-reinforced glass."

Continued Davis: "At least a dozen students over a seven- or eight-year period turned in as part of the collections assignments in undergraduate folklore classes accounts of the ghostly figure who can be classified as a revenant. Not one student admitted to having seen the figure but, as is often the case, students said that they heard the story from a friend of a friend."

And a second eerie tale has evolved from the Morgan murder. Reportedly, on the anniversary of the murder, a bloodstain that soaked into the linoleum floor reappears, despite having been washed away.

"I saw the little laboratory, and I saw the bloodstain, and if I hadn't known what it was I could have mistaken it for anything, just a stain left by something spilled," Davis said. "But one young lady, a sweet sorority girl, said she was so shaken by the story of the darkened bloodstain appearing on the anniversary of the murder, that she refused to enter the [Science] building."

Still another version has a ghost appearing in the top middle window of the former Science Building just before or after the Carol of Lights are switched on.

But Beverly Barnes said her family does not want their grandmother remembered as a spirit that haunts the Science Building. "We know for a fact that this is the last place she'd be," Barnes said in 2014. "She's too busy in heaven, watching all the ones left behind and being loved even still." Barnes died in 2017.

Looking back, the events of December 4, 1967, have also led to a historical perspective.

"I think for a short period of time, it [the murder] probably hurt [student] recruiting," said Dr. Bill Dean, retired Executive Vice President and CEO of the Tech Alumni Association. "The message that came across to me was that there must be great stress and pressure on graduate students, especially in the sciences, to succeed. If [Lach] would kill someone to get access to exams, he was pretty desperate. . . . I seem to recall that the *San Antonio Express-News* had a headline that there was a psychopathic killer roaming this campus. Parents called from everywhere."

"There's no way you can justify what he did," said Larry Hagood, the farmer whose family befriended Benjamin Lach and invited him into their home. "But I wish him well. I hope that he has turned his life around," he added in a 2005 interview. Hagood died in 2022.

"I struggled with how somebody so nice could do something like that," said Walt Hagood, Larry's son, who as a youngster looked up to

On Monday, December 2, 2022, the Carol of Lights event kicked off the beginning of Texas Tech's Centennial Celebration. (Courtesy *Lubbock Avalanche-Journal*.)

Lach. "It changed my perspective—that anything can happen. I used to think that things like that couldn't happen to you, but they can."

The Carol of Lights remains a popular and vibrant holiday tradition at Texas Tech. The sixty-fourth annual event, held on Monday, December 2, 2022, was indeed special, as it kicked off the university's centennial celebration.

Texas Tech president Lawrence Schovanec told the audience that the Carol of Lights is not only a moment to reflect on the history and culture of the university but also a time to look ahead to what it may become. "Our university was born out of a need to serve West Texas and this community," he said.

In addition to a countdown that featured 25,000 LED lights illuminating the campus, a fireworks show was held. The university's combined choirs were joined by the thousands in the crowd in singing Christmas carols, while country musicians the Maines Brothers and Wade Bowen also offered performances. On hand for the festivities as well were the Masked Rider and Raider Red.

The fifty-fifth anniversary of the Alice Morgan murder, which arrived just two days later, passed quietly with no public acknowledgment.

Meanwhile, on December 10, 2022, some 2,000 miles away in a quiet Boston suburb, Benjamin Lach observed his seventy-eighth birthday. His community was listed as the twenty-second best city in which to live in America in 2021, according to a national company that based its ranking of small to mid-sized cities on safety, affordability, economic stability, outdoor recreation, and job opportunities.

Lach was reportedly living a quiet, respectable, and normal life with his wife, a highly respected retired educator/author whom he married in the late 1980s. He operates a wholesale jewelry business out of their residence. They have a daughter and son, both of whom are college graduates. Ironically, the son graduated from Tulane University, the school where the two Tech professors (Kent Rylander and Francis Rose) who played such critical roles in the case earned their doctorates.

Benjamin Lach's brother is a prominent plastic surgeon in the Boston area. Their parents, Herman and Lucy Lach, are deceased. In the 1980s, while living in Brookline, Massachusetts, Lucy was described as a "little blonde lady," while Herman was "burly, and resembled Benjamin."

Had Benjamin Lach served his complete forty-year prison sentence, he would not have been released until March 2008.

He joins others such as James Cross, Jack Brown, Paul Krueger, and James Wolcott (St. John) who were convicted of horrific crimes but who, after confinement, returned to society as productive, law-abiding citizens.

Alice Morgan's husband Richard died in 1996 at age eighty-nine. The elder of their two daughters, Eva Marie Goad, died in 2011 at age eighty, and her sister, Doris Morgan Brewer, died in 2013 at age seventy-four.

SIDEBAR: TECH, ONE OF THE MOST HAUNTED CAMPUSES IN TEXAS

According to *Supernatural Texas—A Field Guide*, published in 2009, Texas Tech is one of the most haunted campuses in the state of Texas. The book lists the following Tech locations as "ghost-sites": Holden Hall, underground steam tunnels, Horn-Knapp Hall, Merket Alumni Center, National Ranching Heritage Center, Thompson Hall, and, interestingly enough, the Biology Building. According to the book, it was in the university's Biology Building (erroneously) where "a custodian named Sarah Morgan surprised a student named Benjamin Cach [*sic*] stealing the answer sheets to the biology exams from one of the third-floor lab rooms."

Darrell Malone's *Haunted Lubbock*, published in 2013, also gives a brief mention of "The Cleaning Lady Murder."

A reference to the crime can even be found in at least two works of fiction, including *My Second Wind—A Novel of Murder, Mystery & Love in Modern-Day West Texas*. Written by Jeanne Guerra (a former Tech employee) in 2013, the book includes the following dialogue between two characters:

"Remember the murder of the cleaning lady a year or so before we came to Tech?"

"Of course. My parents were questioning my choice of schools. Luckily, the guy was caught pretty quickly, wasn't he?"

In this fictional tale, the president's chief of staff is found murdered in the bell tower area of the administration building.

Even more intriguing is a chapter on the crime in *The Mustangs of Cotopaxi and other stories*. This is a collection of short stories published in 2016 by none other than former Tech professor Kent Rylander, whose office Benjamin Lach entered illegally to gain access to exams. The chapter, titled "A Murder in the University," sticks to the basic facts of the case but moves the setting from Texas to California and changes Benjamin's name to Josh.

SIDEBAR: MORE TECH/ LUBBOCK-RELATED MURDERS

Murder has unfortunately surfaced many times through the years in Lubbock and at Texas Tech.

Haskell Taylor, an eighty-three-year-old retired Texas Tech business professor, was beaten and strangled to death in his Lubbock home on October 29, 1996. Taylor was a well-respected Tech professor from 1936 to 1978; to date, the case remains unsolved.

On July 31, 1977, a gruesome murder occurred in Lubbock when Clarence Lackey abducted, raped, and slashed to death twenty-three-year-old Toni Kumpf. The Tech graduate and Texas Tech Health Sciences Center Hospital employee served as an interpreter for Spanish-speaking people. Lackey randomly broke into the woman's apartment, and her body was found nearly decapitated in a Lubbock cotton field.

Nearly twenty years later, on May 20, 1997, the State of Texas executed forty-three-year-old Clarence Lackey by lethal injection.

In recalling the brutal crime, Lubbock Police Capt. Randy Ward offered this comment: "That's when people lost their innocence and started locking their doors," perhaps unaware of the 1967 murder of Alice Morgan.

On January 31, 2001, the bodies of Tech Associate Dean of Libraries Douglas Birdsall and a female companion were found inside a car parked in a drainage gully in Lubbock. Both had died of gunshot wounds. Former Tech architecture student Vaughn Ross was later convicted and sentenced to death for the crime. He was executed in 2013.

And on July 10, 2012, Dr. Joseph Sonnier III was found shot and stabbed to death in his Lubbock home. At the time of his death, Sonnier was medical director for AmeriPath and chief pathologist for Covenant Health System in Lubbock.

Two men, including an Amarillo plastic surgeon, were convicted in a murder-for-hire plot. "It was the most gruesome, high-profile murder Lubbock has ever seen," commented a Lubbock Police Department official.

A tragic murder shook the Tech campus again on October 9, 2017. At approximately 8 p.m., forty-eight-year-old Texas Tech Police officer Floyd East Jr.—a married father of two—was shot to death inside Texas Tech Police Department headquarters (413 Flint Avenue). The department is located on the north perimeter of the expansive Tech campus, north of the Science Building.

Hollis Daniels, a nineteen-year-old Tech freshman from Seguin, Texas, was charged with fatally shooting the officer in police headquarters while being processed for arrest.

After shooting the officer, the suspect fled the scene on foot. With the campus in panic and on lockdown, he was taken into custody around 9:30 p.m. near the Lubbock Municipal Coliseum.

Authorities said that the incident started when Texas Tech police made a student welfare check on the student earlier that evening in his dorm—Talkington Hall (on the south end of campus).

Officers brought Daniels to the police station for standard debriefing. "During this time, the suspect pulled a gun and shot an officer in the head. The officer is deceased," read a statement from the university.

Daniels was held in the Lubbock County Detention Center following his arrest in 2017, and his capital murder case went to trial in February 2023. He entered a plea of guilty, and prosecutors sought the death penalty. After a three-week trial, the jury sentenced Daniels to life without parole.

POSTSCRIPT

Lubbock Police Chief **J. T. Alley** served in that capacity for twenty-five years (November 1957—January 31, 1983). After retiring at age fifty-nine, Alley remained in Lubbock, where he died on April 27, 2009, at age eighty-five.

Bill Bailey, the Lubbock police officer who handcuffed Benjamin Lach at Resthaven Cemetery, died in Lubbock on June 10, 1997, at age sixty-four.

F. Lee Bailey, a native of Waltham, Massachusetts, and a famed criminal defense attorney, was contacted prior to the Lach trial but did not take the case. He had earlier defended Albert DeSalvo in the Boston Strangler case, and many years later was part of the O. J. Simpson defense team. Bailey died in Atlanta, Georgia, on June 3, 2021, at age eighty-seven.

In an ironic twist of fate, Lubbock psychiatrist **Dr. Louis Barnes**, who had testified at Lach's original sanity hearing, was deceased by the time the second hearing was held. Barnes, forty-three, was stabbed to death in his Lubbock home on September 24, 1969. Just after Lach was transported from Rusk State Hospital back to Lubbock, **Madeline Barnes**, the psychiatrist's wife, was sent to Rusk. She was charged with her husband's murder and ruled mentally incompetent to stand trial. On June 17, 1971, Mrs. Barnes was returned to Lubbock, where she was ruled competent to stand trial. She had received psychiatric treatment on two occasions since 1950 and was released from hospitals against the advice of doctors. Madeline Barnes died on December 4, 1976, in El Paso, Texas, at age forty-six.

Tom Barnes was a Texas Department of Public Safety polygraph examiner who administered polygraphs to Benjamin Lach on two separate occasions. He began his law enforcement career as a patrolman with the Lubbock Police Department in the 1940s. Barnes retired from the DPS in 1977, then worked in the private polygraph business until 1994. He died in Lubbock on March 20, 1995, at the age of seventy-one.

Carrol G. (C. G.) Bartley, a Lubbock Police captain, along with District Attorney Alton Griffin, was present for Benjamin Lach's confession. He joined the department in 1961 and served as assistant police chief in the late 1970s–1980s.

Dr. Julian Biggers Jr. was acting assistant dean of the School of Education at Texas Tech in 1967. He was the first person to notice a likeness between Benjamin Lach and a composite drawing distributed by law enforcement. He taught at Tech from 1966 to 1992 and is now professor of educational psychology and leadership, emeritus. Prior to his tenure at Tech, Biggers was employed by the Texas Education Agency (Division of Guidance Services).

Bart Blaydes was a Texas Tech student who testified he saw a man other than Benjamin Lach in the basement of the Science Building on the night of the Morgan murder. Blaydes taught horticulture for thirty-three years at Richland College in Dallas, retiring in 2009.

Doris Barnett Brewer, the younger daughter of Richard and Sarah Alice Morgan, died in Marietta, Oklahoma, on February 23, 2013, at age seventy-four.

Dolphus Jack Brown, convicted of murdering his parents in Shallowater, Texas, in 1967, was quickly cleared of any involvement in the Alice Morgan murder. Brown was sentenced to thirteen years in prison for the murder of his parents. He served five years, from March 1972 to May 1977, and was then paroled. Later in life, he was a successful business owner in Texas. He died in a traffic accident on July 8, 2012, in Eustace, Texas. At the time of his death, he was a resident of LaRue, Texas. He was seventy.

Lubbock patrolman **Emmett Caddell**, who spotted Benjamin Lach in a stolen car and chased him into Resthaven Cemetery, died in Anton, Texas, on November 11, 2010, at age eighty-five.

Dr. Earl Camp was chair of the biology department at Texas Tech from 1959 to 1970 and taught there from 1945 to 1985. He died on July 2, 2006, in Lubbock, at age eighty-eight.

Judge J. Blair Cherry Jr. retired on January 31, 2006, as Judge of the 72nd District Court in Lubbock after seventeen years on the bench and took the role of senior district judge. At the time of the Morgan murder, he was first assistant Lubbock County district attorney and was later elected Lubbock County district attorney. Alton Griffin and Cherry co-prosecuted Lach. He died on August 18, 2023, in Fort Worth, at age 84.

Bill Cox, Lubbock chief of police detectives, joined the department in 1950 and served for thirty-five years. He died in Lubbock on October 8, 2005, at age eighty-four.

Judge Carl Dally was an appeals attorney for Benjamin Lach and later served as a judge in the Texas Court of Criminal Appeals from 1978 to 1983. Prior to taking Lach's appeals case, Dally was a Harris County assistant district attorney for six years. He died on October 19, 2022, at age ninety-eight.

Bill Daniels was Texas Tech's first police chief, serving in that capacity from 1959 until retirement in 1986. The Shallowater County native was a US Army paratrooper during the Normandy Invasion. Before joining the Tech police force, Daniels was employed by the Lubbock Police Department, Lubbock Sheriff's Department, and Slaton Police Department. He died in Lubbock on November 28, 1996, at age seventy-four.

Dawson "Doss" Davis was a prosecutor in Fort Worth in the 1950s and was later appointed as a public defender to assist with the defense at the Benjamin Lach murder trial in Fort Worth. He died in Fort Worth on April 19, 1980, at age eighty-one.

Dr. Kenneth Davis was a professor of English at Texas Tech from 1960 to 1994 and then professor emeritus. He died in Lubbock in 2019, at age eighty-six.

Judge Howard Davison of the 99th District Court served in that capacity from 1960 to 1974. He presided over Benjamin Lach's sanity hearings and later, in the capital murder case, granted the defense a change of venue to Fort Worth. He died in Lubbock on December 3, 1990, at age eighty.

Dr. Bill Dean was director of student publications at Texas Tech from 1967 to 1978, and from 1978 to 2018 he served as executive vice president and CEO of the Texas Tech Alumni Association. He continued teaching at Tech until 2021, retiring after fifty-four years of service to the institution.

Joan Dominick was a Texas Tech student who befriended Benjamin Lach and testified that Lach was with her at the time of the murder. She died in Lubbock on May 9, 2003, at age sixty-two.

Ray Downing, director of building maintenance at Texas Tech and who played a key role in the Carol of Lights in the 1960s, died in Lubbock in 1973 at age fifty-five.

Marilyn Ehrlich, a Texas Tech graduate student in 1967, testified that while in the Science Building on the night of the murder, she talked to Alice Morgan and also saw Benjamin Lach nearby.

Duncan Ellison was the KLBK-TV news director in 1967 who took photographs of persons of interest at the funeral of Alice Morgan. He died in Lubbock on November 18, 1994, at the age of seventy-one.

James Fergerson was a Lubbock Police captain who was among the Alice Morgan crime scene investigators. He began working for the Lubbock PD in November 1950 and retired in 2004. He died on June 14, 2010, in Lubbock, at the age of eighty-three.

J. D. Fortner was a Texas Tech police sergeant at the time of the Morgan slaying. The Arkansas native also worked for the Lubbock Sheriff's Department and Lubbock Police Department. He retired as acting police chief at Texas Tech in 1988 and returned to Arkansas to work as a truck driver. He died in Jacksonville, Arkansas, on February 21, 2013, at age seventy-eight.

Roy Furr was chairman of the Texas Tech Board of Regents in 1967. He was CEO of Furr Supermarkets & Cafeterias. Furr died in Lubbock on June 11, 1975, at age sixty-nine.

Herschel Garner was a Texas Tech student at the time of the Morgan murder. He identified Benjamin Lach as walking up the stairs to the third floor in the Science Building on the night of the slaying. Garner is professor emeritus of biological sciences at Tarleton State University, where he taught from 1970 to 1996.

William J. "Bill" Gillespie was a court-appointed defense co-counsel for Benjamin Lach. He had served as Lubbock County attorney in the late 1950s and entered private practice in 1960. He died in 1978, at age fifty-one.

Dr. Robert Glen was a Dallas psychologist who testified for the defense in the Benjamin Lach trial. He is deceased.

Eva Marie Goad was the older daughter of Richard and Sarah Alice Morgan. She worked for many years as a cashier at the Methodist Hospital cafeteria in Lubbock. Goad died in Lubbock on September 20, 2011, at age eighty.

James Granberry, the former Lubbock orthodontist, city councilman, mayor, gubernatorial candidate, and parole board member, died in Hideaway, Texas, on March 5, 2021, at age eighty-eight.

Alton Griffin was Lubbock County district attorney at the time of the Morgan murder and later appointed as special prosecutor in the Benjamin Lach murder trial. He served as a prosecutor from 1956 to 1978, except for three years when he was in private practice. Griffin held positions of assistant Lubbock County attorney, Lubbock County attorney, Lubbock County district attorney, and Lubbock County criminal district attorney. He maintained a law office in Lubbock until his death on January 24, 2006, at age seventy-nine.

Larry Hagood was a Tahoka, Texas, farmer and real estate businessman whose family befriended Benjamin Lach prior to the murder. He died in Lubbock in 2022 at age ninety-two.

Phil Hamilton, *Lubbock Avalanche-Journal* reporter, is deceased.

F. C. "Butch" Hargrave was a Lubbock police detective involved in the stakeout of Dr. Kent Rylander's office in the Texas Tech Science Building. He spent twenty-six years in law enforcement, retiring in 1987. Hargrave ran unsuccessfully for Lubbock County Sheriff. He died in Plano, Texas, on December 30, 2011, at age seventy-four.

Jay Harris was a longtime editor of the *Lubbock Avalanche-Journal*, where his career spanned fifty-three years. He died in Lubbock on February 26, 2006, at age eighty-seven.

John C. Hightower, foreman of the custodial department at Texas Tech in the 1960s, retired in 1970. He died in Lubbock in 1976 at age seventy-three.

Dr. John A. Hunter was the Rusk State Hospital physician who examined Benjamin Lach during his stay there. He retired in 1987 and died in Rusk on October 28, 2001, at age eighty-five.

Sal Ingenere was the assistant district attorney in Boston who visited Lubbock in a futile attempt to question Benjamin Lach about a similar murder in the Boston area. He died in Massachusetts on November 14, 1995, at age seventy-nine.

Frank Judd and **David Schmidly**, the two graduate teaching assistants and officemates who unsuccessfully tried to enter Room 304-J during the Morgan murder, went on to distinguished careers in the academic world. Judd, who was twenty-eight years old at the time of the murder, died in 2020 at age eighty-one. He was a retired research professor of biology at University of Texas–Pan American. At the time of the murder, Schmidly was twenty-three years old. He completed his master's degree requirements at Tech in 1968 and continued his studies at the University of Illinois, where he earned his PhD in zoology.

Schmidly served as the thirteenth president of Texas Tech University (2000–2002). Prior to serving as president at Tech, Schmidly was vice president and dean of the graduate school at the university. He also spent twenty-five years in various positions at Texas A&M University. Schmidly left Tech on November 25, 2002, to become president of Oklahoma State University and CEO of the OSU System. In early 2007, Schmidly accepted the position of president at the University of New Mexico. He retired in 2012; that same year, Texas Tech honored Schmidly with its Distinguished Alumnus Award.

Dave Knapp was a *Lubbock Avalanche-Journal* special assignments and police reporter in 1967. He was a key figure in working with the authorities in determining Benjamin Lach as a murder suspect and in the subsequent stakeout of Dr. Kent Rylander's office. He spent twenty-seven years at the *A-J*, eventually promoted to the positions of managing editor and executive editor. While there, he won numerous awards and was nominated twice for a Pulitzer Prize. In 1990, he became chief operating officer of Knapp Communications, a marketing-advertising firm founded by his wife and located near Houston (The Woodlands). He died in The Woodlands on February 3, 2013, at age eighty-one.

Dr. Murray Kovnar was a Texas Tech clinical psychologist from 1961 to 1971. He examined Benjamin Lach and recommended that he be confined to Rusk State Hospital. He died in Lubbock on October 17, 1971, at age fifty-nine.

Judge Wayne LeCroy was Lubbock County Precinct 6 Justice of the Peace for fifteen years, beginning in 1967, and presided over Benjamin Lach's examining trial. He had twelve years of service with the Lubbock Police Department and worked as district clerk for twelve years. He died in Lubbock on January 25, 2004, at age seventy-one.

Dr. Harold L. "Hal" Lewis joined the Tech faculty in 1965. The assistant biology professor told authorities that he had registered Benjamin Lach for the spring 1968 semester. He also said that he had seen Lach on more than one occasion in the north attic of the Science Building, although not on the night of the murder. Lewis left Tech to become manager of physiology and biochemistry research for the National Cotton Council in Tennessee. He died in Conway, Arkansas, on January 30, 2015, at age eighty.

Macie Mathis was a custodian at Texas Tech for fifteen years. Mathis, who discovered her coworker and friend Alice Morgan's body, died in Slaton, Texas, on December 26, 2000, at age ninety-one.

Byron Matthews served as judge of the Criminal District Court Number One in Tarrant County from 1963 to 1981. He was the judge in the murder trial of Benjamin Lach. He was a member of the Texas Criminal Defense Lawyers Hall of Fame. Matthews died in Fort Worth on November 3, 2006, at age ninety-four.

Kenneth May served as associate editor of the *Lubbock Avalanche-Journal* and as a civic leader until his death on July 3, 1989, at the age of fifty-nine.

Roy McQueen, a *University Daily* co-managing editor in 1967, was owner and publisher of the *Snyder Daily News* for many years. He is retired.

John T. Montford, while serving as Lubbock County district attorney and state senator, frequently objected to Benjamin Lach's parole bids. The former Texas Tech Chancellor now owns a consulting business.

Richard "Ocie" Morgan, the husband of murder victim Alice Morgan, died in Lubbock on December 13, 1996, at age ninety-six.

Dr. Grover Murray, who had a distinguished career as Texas Tech president from 1966 to 1976, died on May 22, 2003, at age eighty-six.

Dr. Richard K. O'Loughlin, a Lubbock psychiatrist who examined Benjamin Lach, died in Lubbock on February 23, 1973, at age fifty-six.

Dr. John P. Ray, a Lubbock pathologist who performed an autopsy on Alice Morgan, died in 1984 at the age of fifty-eight.

Dr. Francis Rose, the professor in whose lab Alice Morgan was murdered, eventually departed Lubbock to become a professor of biology at Southwest Texas State University (now Texas State University). Rose is professor emeritus at Texas State.

Dr. Kent Rylander was the Texas Tech biology professor whose office was the scene of a stakeout in which one of his students, Benjamin Lach, entered with a stolen key. After thirty-nine years of teaching, Rylander retired from Tech in 2004 and has written several books since that time.

A. W. Salyars, the colorful attorney on the court-appointed defense team of Benjamin Lach, served as a district attorney for five years before opening a private practice in Lubbock in 1947. He died in Lubbock on September 18, 1996, at age eighty.

Boston police **Lt. Edward Sherry** came to Lubbock in an attempt to question Benjamin Lach regarding a murder in Massachusetts. He retired in 1973 after thirty-four years as a policeman, investigating 1,500 slayings. He died in Portland, Maine, on February 27, 1975, at age sixty.

Bob Tedder, a Lubbock police sergeant involved in the Alice Morgan murder investigation, died in Lubbock on October 4, 1975, at age forty-one.

Kenneth Ray Vaughn, the first Lubbock police officer to arrive at the scene of the Morgan murder, had a thirty-seven-year career in law enforcement, including stints with the Lubbock Police Department and Lubbock County Sheriff's Office. He died in Lubbock on September 2, 2014, at age seventy-six.

Detective **Frank Wiley**, who along with Butch Hargrave staked out Kent Rylander's office, served the Lubbock Police Department for thirty-nine years, retiring in 1996. Wiley was assistant chief of police of the detective division during the last two years of his career. He died in Lubbock on December 31, 2010, at age seventy-seven.

ACKNOWLEDGMENTS

Tom Akins
Blake Allen
Ed Bernd
Dr. Walter Borst
Michelle Burton
Judge J. Blair Cherry
Dr. Bryon Clark
Dr. Kenneth Davis
Dr. Bill Dean
Perry Flippin
Larry Hagood
Walt Hagood
Floyd "Butch" Hargrave
David Keeling
Judith Keeling
Mary Jo Keeling
Wayne Keeling
Debbie Lane
Chuck Lanehart
Gary Lavergne
Roy McQueen

J. Weston Marshall,
    Texas Tech University
    Southwest Collection/Special
    Collections Library
Sharon Morrison
Ronnie Perry
Kathryn Plunkett
DeAnn Prince
Tom Purdom
Lesley Reeves,
    The Windsor Agency
Dr. Kent Rylander
Nana Rylander
Randy Sanders,
    Lubbock Avalanche-Journal
President David Schmidly
José Silva Jr.
Debbie Smith
Jackie Smith
Joe Smith
Southeastern Oklahoma

State University Henry
Bennett Library
Barbara Sucsy
Texas Tech University Library
Lynn Whitfield,
  Texas Tech University
  Southwest Collection/Special
  Collections Library
Frank Wiley
Jim Willett,
  Texas Prison Museum
Adam Young,
  Lubbock Avalanche-Journal

AUTHORS' NOTES

WHEN ALICE MORGAN WAS MURDERED AT TEXAS Tech in December 1967, I was in Mrs. Brown's fifth grade class at Fairview Elementary School in the North Texas town of Sherman. At that time, little did I know that nine years later, I would be a student at Texas Tech University, frequently walking past the scene (Science Building) of the crime on my way to class and living nearby (Murdough Hall, and later at the Honeycomb Apartments). While at Tech, I heard whispered rumors about the tragedy, but little else.

I have mostly fond memories of Tech, notwithstanding the semiannual endurance of lengthy class registration lines at Municipal Coliseum. Time tends to dim our recollections and inflate our GPAs, but I do recall a memorable line uttered by one of my professors, when noting the propensity of Tech students to skip Friday classes in order to perfect the art of skiing in nearby New Mexico: "If Tech students were going to hell," the bearded young business prof told us, "they'd leave a day early."

One other memorable experience at Tech involved meeting a thirty-two-year-old unknown oilman from Midland named George W. Bush. The future governor and president was in Lubbock campaigning in his first political race, hoping to replace longtime West Texas congressman George Mahon.

In order to attract the Tech student vote, the brash, charismatic, and affable Bush advertised—in the student newspaper—a free beer bash, which, we thought, from the students' perspective, was a brilliant strategic move. (At that point, eighteen-year-olds could both legally vote and drink alcohol, though ideally not at the same time.)

For some reason, my roommate and I showed up just as the event was ending in a field on a cold, windy afternoon. We hesitated, seeing only two men still there, but walked up to them anyway. Wearing a heavy overcoat, the future Governor of Texas and President of the United States looked me directly in the eye, shook my hand firmly, and made this unforgettable remark: "Shit, it's cold out here."

Alas, Bush's beer bash was bashed by his opponent's (Kent Hance) camp. Hance insisted to the local Church of Christ affiliates that his opponent had certainly ruined the morals of the previously innocent Tech students. Bush was then narrowly defeated by Hance (a conservative Democrat in 1978 and later the Tech chancellor and a conservative Republican). It proved to be the only political race that Bush ever lost.

One ironic note concerning the date (December 4, 1967) of the Texas Tech slaying: earlier that same day, a twenty-nine-year-old Sherman housewife was found lying outside of her home just southeast of town. She had been raped and stabbed eight times and died later that afternoon. Such horrific crimes were not infrequent sixty miles to the south in big-city Dallas. But a murder in small-town Sherman (population 26,000) in 1967 was indeed rare; for the most part, we experienced life through a *Leave It to Beaver* lens. Sadly, this signaled the beginning of a more violent time for our residents. Over the next two and a half years, two young schoolgirls, one in Sherman and one in neighboring Denison, were abducted on their way home from school and murdered. Also during this time, a Sherman police officer and service station attendant were shot to death during an early morning robbery.

In regard to the 1967 murder of the housewife, a twenty-one-year-old Sherman man was arrested the following month and eventually convicted of the brutal crime.

On December 17, 1968, the perpetrator pled guilty and was sentenced to life in prison by Judge James Zimmermann of the Criminal District Court No. 3 in Dallas. After forty-two years behind bars, the man was discharged in October 2010. A couple of years after the murder, Texas Ranger Lewis Rigler noted that the killer "was such a quiet, unobtrusive person that even his neighbors were startled when they had learned he had confessed to the rape-slaying."

Just a day later, on December 18, 1968, twenty-four-year-old Benjamin Lach was found insane by a Lubbock jury and sent to Rusk State Hospital.

On the day of the Lubbock and Sherman murders, I was just about to turn eleven years old. The Sherman case was the first real murder that I was really aware of as a child, at least in my hometown.

I had no hidden agenda in writing *Fatal Exam: Solving Lubbock's Greatest Murder Mystery* other than to provide a factual and historical account of a tragic event that was, while gruesome, most unusual in its twists and turns through the years. As is often said, truth is stranger than fiction, and this case is a prime example. It is also not my intent to cast a negative light on Texas Tech or any individual or group.

This book is the result of extensive research, interviews, and visits to Lubbock spanning twenty years. The research began with a simple written request to the Tech Library for copies of all newspaper articles pertinent to the murder case. From there, I journeyed to Lubbock for a similar request to Randy Sanders, then-editor of the *Lubbock Avalanche-Journal*. As the book notes, the *A-J* played a key role in solving the case—Sanders could not have been more gracious in permitting me access to the newspaper's archives, while also allowing me use of photographs. Also of assistance was former newspaper editor Perry Flippin, for whom I worked many years ago at the *Sherman Democrat*. *A-J* editor Adam Young was also kind enough to grant permission to use photos.

A great deal of thanks also goes to J. Weston Marshall and everyone at the Texas Tech University Southwest Collection/Special Collections Library for their tireless assistance.

I was allowed to obtain copies of official police reports and court documents relevant to the case—thanks are in order to the late Judge J. Blair Cherry Jr. and John Grace, then with the Lubbock County Criminal District Attorney's Office and who was elected Judge in the 72nd District Court in Lubbock in 2022.

Thanks are also due to the late Sharon Morrison, who served as library director at Southeastern Oklahoma State University for many years, who made arrangements for the loaning of college catalogs for my use from the Texas Tech Library. And to Jim Willett of the Texas Prison Museum, who graciously granted me access to archives of *The Echo* newspaper.

I want to acknowledge the Keeling family of Lubbock for their support and hospitality during my frequent research trips to West Texas.

And a special thanks to Dr. Walter Borst, professor emeritus of physics and astronomy at Texas Tech, for his research and assistance, and to the Hagood family for their insight.

This book could not have been written without the tireless cooperation of the late Judge Cherry and the late Alton Griffin—both of these gentlemen were kind, patient, and invaluable resources, and I had the pleasure of interviewing them in person on more than one occasion. I know it had to be awkward for them (and others) when someone they did not know contacted them out of the blue, inquiring about an unpleasant event that had occurred almost forty years earlier. Judge Cherry spent a great deal of time providing details and anecdotes, while leading me to additional sources during the lengthy research phase of the book. I had nothing but the utmost respect for Judge Cherry, who died in August 2023.

In addition to Judge Cherry and Mr. Griffin, I thank all the other persons who agreed to be interviewed for this book. For the record, I conducted the interviews through a variety of methods, including in-person, telephone, and by email.

I also respect the wishes of those few individuals who declined my request for interviews.

The authors attempted to contact Benjamin Lach with written questions on two occasions but never received a response from him. We can only assume that he did not wish to be interviewed for this book, and again, we respect his decision.

A word of thanks also goes to my co-author Chuck Lanehart, who provided much-needed insight and perspective along with his writing and legal expertise.

Finally, my co-author and I express our gratitude to Travis Snyder, editor in chief at Texas Tech University Press, for believing in and supporting the book; Carly Kahl, our talented copy editor; Senior Editor Christie Perlmutter for proofreading the galleys; Senior Designer Hannah Gaskamp for the striking book design; and Marketing Manager John Brock for promotion and sales. I will be forever grateful to former Texas Tech Press editor Judith Keeling, who gave me the first opportunity to be published many years ago. *Fatal Exam: Solving Lubbock's Greatest Murder Mystery* has been twenty years in the making, and my sincere hope is that the end result reflects the amount of time, research, thought, and effort that went into its creation.

ALAN BURTON

I was pleased and surprised when a stranger, Alan Burton, contacted me about collaborating on his book about the Benjamin Lach case. I had published an article about the case in the *Lubbock Avalanche-Journal*'s "Caprock Chronicles" column, and the article was also part of my book, *Tragedy and Triumph on the Texas Plains*. Alan had seen the article and thought I might be interested in his project. He came to Lubbock, we bonded over lunch, and I agreed to co-author this volume.

I was impressed by Alan's work on the project, which spanned many years. He had done an enormous amount of thorough research and thoughtful writing, so I felt guilty about my name appearing on the book cover, but not guilty enough to turn down an opportunity to have my name attached to such an interesting and important chronicle of history.

Even though I became licensed to practice law in 1977, well after the Lach trial, I was privileged to have known almost all the important characters in the Lach drama: educators Grover Murray and Bill Dean, cops Bill Daniels and Butch Hargrave, criminal defense lawyers Bill Gillespie and Shorty Salyars, prosecutors Blair Cherry and Alton Griffin, judges Wayne LeCroy and Howard Davison, and many of the newspapermen (as I am a recovering journalist). Some of these folks became my close friends. I was pleased to be able to contribute my personal knowledge of these fellows in order to augment Alan's previous research. There were a few tricky bits of law, legal procedure, and legalese that I helped put in perspective for readers.

From my previous historical research on this and other topics, I was in possession of a number of photos associated with the story, so I was able to provide those to the project as well. Many of the photos had originally been obtained from the Southwest Collection at Texas Tech University and the *Lubbock Avalanche-Journal*. I thank SWC uber-archivists Monte Monroe and Weston Marshall and *A-J* editor Adam Young and his predecessors for their assistance.

I am a full-time criminal defense trial lawyer, but writing is one of my passions. I could not have kept my law practice going while devoting time to this book had it not been for the assistance of my brilliant law partner Fred Stangl and our dedicated office staff: Bernadette Vaughn, Tiffany Neal, and Angie Carroll.

CHUCK LANEHART

REFERENCES

BOOKS, MAGAZINE ARTICLES, SELECTED NEWSPAPER ARTICLES, REPORTS, FURTHER READING

Allen, Dana, Regina Bouley, Paula Khalaf, James Ridgway, Haley Stoner, Daniel Stryker, Cami Whitehead, eds. *Voices from Texas Death Row*. Huntsville, TX: Texas Review Press, 2009.

Amburn, Ellis. *Buddy Holly: A Biography*. New York: St. Martin's Press, 1995.

Andrews, Ruth Horn. *The First Thirty Years—1925—A History of Texas Technological College—1955*. Lubbock: Texas Tech Press, 1956.

Barefoot, Daniel W. *Haunted Hall of Ivy: Ghosts of Southern Colleges and Universities*. Winston-Salem, NC: John F. Blair Publisher, 2004.

Barer, Burl. *Fatal Beauty*. New York: Kensington Publishing Co., 2011.

Barrick, Nolan E. *Texas Tech: The Unobserved History*. Lubbock: Texas Tech University Press, 1985.

Baskerville, Allyn, and Bill Gillespie. *Honk If You Love J. Edgar Hoover*. Orlando, FL: First Publish, 2001.

Beattie, Robert. *Language of Evil*. New York: Signet Books, 2009.

Berry-Dee, Christopher. *Psychopaths: Up Close and Personal. Inside the Minds of Sociopaths, Serial Killers and Deranged Murderers*. Berkeley, CA: Ulysses Press, 2017.

Biggers, Dr. Julian. *The School Counselor at Work*. Austin: Texas Education Agency, 1968.

Bobonich, Chris. *Bloody Ivy: 13 Unsolved Campus Murders*. Bloomington, IN: AuthorHouse, 2013.

Boen, Hannah. "Ghost Hunters Visit Tech Campus." *Daily Toreador*, October 30, 2008.

Brown, Alan. *Haunted Southwest*. Haunted America Series. Cheltenham, UK: The History Press, 2016.

Brown, Pat. *Killing for Sport: Inside the Minds of Serial Killers*. Beverly Hills, CA: New Millennium Press, 2003.

Buss, David M. *The Murderer Next Door. Why the Mind Is Designed to Kill*. New York: Penguin Books, 2005.

Capote, Truman. *In Cold Blood*. New York: Random House, 1965.

Carr, Joe, and Alan Munde. *Prairie Nights to Neon Lights: The Story of Country Music in West Texas*. Lubbock: Texas Tech University Press, 1995.

Cartwright, Chad. *Shock*. Self-published, 2013.

Cartwright, Gary. *Confessions of a Washed-Up Sportswriter: Including Various Digressions About Sex, Crime, and Other Hobbies*. Austin: Texas Monthly Press, 1982.

Casey, Kathryn. *A Descent into Hell: The True Story of an Altar Boy, A Cheerleader, and a Twisted Texas Murder*. New York: Harper Books, 2008.

Cash, Wanda Garner, and Ed Sterling, eds. *The News in Texas: Essays in Honor of the 125th Anniversary of the Texas Press Association*. The Center for American History, University of Texas at Austin. Austin: University of Texas Press, 2005.

Cleckley, Hervey. *The Mask of Sanity: An Attempt to Clarify Some Issues about the So-Called Psychopathic Personality*. Augusta, GA: C. V. Mosby Co., 1988.

Cochran, Mike. "Gotta Lub It." *Fort Worth Star-Telegram*, November 2002.

Cochran, Mike, and John Lumpkin. *West Texas: A Portrait of Its People and Their Raw and Wondrous Land.* Lubbock: Texas Tech University Press, 1999.

The Committee on Nomenclature and Statistics of the American Psychiatric Association. "Diagnostic and Statistical Manual of Mental Disorders (DSM—II)." 2nd ed. Washington, DC: American Psychiatric Association, 1968.

Cooper, Becky. *We Keep the Dead Close: A Murder at Harvard and a Half Century of Silence.* New York: Grand Central Publishing, 2020.

Crawford, Bill. *Texas Death Row: Executions in the Modern Era.* New York: Plume, 2008.

Dean, Bill. "Unsettling Events: Yesterday and Today." *Texas Techsan,* March/April 2005.

DeKok, David. *Murder in the Stacks: Penn State, Betsy Aardsma, and the Killer Who Got Away.* Guilford, CT: Globe Pequot Press, 2014.

Draper, W. D. "History of Administration Building Rusk State Hospital."

Drummond, Paul. *Eye Mind: The Saga of Roky Erickson and the 13th Floor Elevators, the Pioneers of Psychedelic Sound.* Los Angeles, CA: Process Media, 2007.

Ely, Joe. *Reverb: An Odyssey.* Lubbock: Lettersat3amPress, 2014.

Ethier, Eric. *True Crime: Massachusetts: The State's Most Notorious Criminal Cases.* Mechanicsburg, PA: Stackpole Books, 2009.

Evans, Wanda, and James Dunn. *Trail of Blood: A Father, a Son and a Tell-Tale Crime Scene Investigation.* Far Hills, NJ: New Horizon Press, 2005.

Fero, Kelly. *The Zani Murders.* New York: Dell Books, 1990.

Fox, James, and Jack Levin. *Killer on Campus: The Terrifying True Story of the Gainesville Ripper.* New York: Avon Books, 1996.

Francis, Eric. *The Dartmouth Murders.* New York: St. Martin's Press, 2002.

Frank, Gerald. *The Boston Strangler.* New York: New American Library, 1966.

Gaffney, Michael. "Tech Folklorist Knows Where the Ghosts are

Haunting." Lubbock Online.com, October 2004.

Gaylin, Willard. *The Killing of Bonnie Garland: A Question of Justice.* New York: Penguin Books, 1983.

Glenn, Lon Bennett. *Texas Prison Tales: The Largest Hotel Chain in Texas II.* CreateSpace, 2016.

———. *Texas Prisons: The Largest Hotel Chain in Texas.* Austin: Eakin Press, 2001.

Golding, Jack, Phil Hamilton, Jay Harris, and Dave Knapp. *The Lubbock Tornado.* Lubbock: Boone Publications, 1970.

Goldrosen, John. *The Buddy Holly Story.* Bowling Green, OH: The Bowling Green University Popular Press, 1975.

Graves, Lawrence, ed. *Lubbock from Town to City.* Lubbock: West Texas Museum Association, 1986.

Griggs, Brian. *Opus in Brick and Stone: The Architectural and Planning Heritage of Texas Tech University.* Lubbock: Texas Tech University Press, 2020.

Guerra, Jeanne S. *My Second Wind: A Novel of Murder, Mystery & Love in Modern-Day West Texas.* CreateSpace, 2013.

Guttmacher, Manfred. *The Mind of the Murderer.* New York: Grove Press, Inc., 1962.

Hare, Robert D. *Without Conscience: The Disturbing World of the Psychopaths Among Us.* New York: The Guilford Press, 1993.

Harper, William. *Eleven Days in Hell: The 1974 Carrasco Prison Siege at Huntsville, Texas.* Denton: University of North Texas Press, 2004.

Hill, Russell. *Lubbock.* Postcard History series. Charleston, SC: Arcadia Publishing, 2011.

Hinckley, Jack, Jo Ann Hinckley, with Elizabeth Sherrill. *Breaking Points.* Guideposts edition. Carmel, NY: Zondervan Publishing, 1985.

Horton, Bob. *Of Bulletins and Booze: A Newsman's Story of Recovery.* Lubbock: Texas Tech University Press, 2017.

Horton, David M., and George R. Nielsen. *Walking George: The Life of George John Beto and the Rise of the Modern Texas Prison System.* Denton: University of North Texas Press, 2005.

Hubbard, Bill. *Substantial Evidence*. Far Hills, NJ: New Horizon Press, 2007.

Hugunin, James R. *A Survey of the Representation of Prisoners in the United States: Discipline and Photographs, The Prison Experience*. Lewiston, NY: Edwin Mellen Press, 1999.

Jones, James. "Lach Named Echo Editor." *The Echo* (Huntsville, TX), February 1975.

Judd, Frank W., and Francis L. Rose. *The Texas Tortoise: A Natural History*. Norman: University of Oklahoma Press, 2014.

Junger, Sebastian. *A Death in Belmont*. New York: Harper Perennial, 2007.

Kerr, Gordon. *Mapping the Trail of a Crime: How Experts Use Geographic Profiling to Solve the World's Most Notorious Cases*. New York: Reader's Digest Press, 2011.

Keyes, Edward. *The Michigan Murders*. New York: Reader's Digest Press, 1976.

King, Danielle Yoshiko. "More Than a Ghost Story: The Real Story of the Murder at Texas Tech." Blog. Wordpress, June 10, 2014, and November 17, 2015.

Knapp, Dave. "Tech Slayer Eager for Parole." *Lubbock Avalanche-Journal*, April 18, 1976.

Lavergne, Gary M. *Bad Boy from Rosebud: The Murderous Life of Kenneth Allen McDuff*. Denton: University of North Texas Press, 1999.

———. *A Sniper in the Tower: The Charles Whitman Murders*. Denton: University of North Texas Press, 1997.

LaVoie Megan, Justin Vallejo, and Nikki Siegrist. "Campus Is Home to Several Haunts." *Daily Toreador*, October 31, 2003.

Legislative Budget Board Staff. "Managing and Funding State Mental Hospitals in Texas." Legislative Primer, submitted to the 82nd Texas Legislature, Austin, Texas, February 2011.

Looney, Douglas S. "Inside Slant on the Colleges." *Sports Illustrated*, September 5, 1984.

Luck, Carol Lynn. *Gym Class Klutz*. CreateSpace, 2016.

———. *Heroines of the Kitchen Table: Stories of Survivors*. CreateSpace, 2014.

———. *Magnolias Don't Bloom in September*. Golden Pages Press, 2019.

Maddox, Bill. *The Other Side of the Camera*. Maitland, FL: Xulon Press, 2014.

Mahoney, J. Michael. *Schizophrenia: The Bearded Lady Disease*. Bloomington, IN: First Books Library, 2006.

Malcolm, Janet. *The Journalist and the Murderer*. New York: Vintage Books, 1990.

Maloney, Darrell. *Haunted Lubbock: True Ghost Stories from the Hub of the Plains*. CreateSpace, 2013.

Martin, Steve J., and Sheldon Ekland-Olson. *Texas Prisons: The Walls Came Tumbling Down*. Austin: Texas Monthly Press, 1987.

May, Kymberli. "School of Scares." La Vida section of *Daily Toreador*. Lubbock, Texas, October 27, 2006.

Maysel, Lou. *Here Come the Texas Longhorns: 1893–1970*. Fort Worth: Stadium Publishing Company, 1970.

McAleer, Dave. *The Book of Hit Singles: Top 20 Charts, from 1954 to the Present Day*. San Francisco, CA: Backbeat Books, 2001.

McGinniss, Joe. *Fatal Vision*. New York: Signet Books, 1984.

McKinley, Fred. *A Plea for Justice: The Timothy Cole Story*. Austin: Eakin Press, 2010.

McVay, Freda. *The Paradoxical Plainsman: A Biography of the (More or Less) Honorable Chas. A. Guy*. Lubbock: Texas Tech Press, 1983.

Meyer, Peter. *The Yale Murder: The Compelling True Narrative of the Fatal Romance of Bonnie Garland and Richard Herrin*. New York: Empire Books, 1982.

Michaud, Stephen G., with Roy Hazelwood. *The Evil That Men Do: FBI Profiler Roy Hazelwood's Journey into the Minds of Sexual Predators*. New York: St. Martin's Paperbacks, 2000.

Mintz, Ruth Finer. *Modern Hebrew Poetry: A Bilingual Anthology*. Berkeley, CA: University of California Press, 1966.

Minutaglio, Bill. *First Son: George W. Bush and the Bush Family Dynasty*. New York: Three Rivers Press, 2001.

Mitchell, Corey. *Murdered Innocents*. New York: Kensington Publishing

Company, 2005.

Mitchell, Jerry. *"The Fifth Asylum": Rusk State Hospital, 1919–1991.* Unpublished manuscript, 1987, 1991.

Moffitt, William Alan. "Law Enforcement in Lubbock, Texas: A Study of Intergovernmental Relations." Master's thesis, Texas Tech University, 1968.

Morris, James McGrath. *Jailhouse Journalism: The Fourth Estate Behind Bars.* New Brunswick, NJ: Transaction Publishers, 2002.

Morris, Rebecca. *A Murder in My Hometown.* Denver, CO: Wildblue Press, 2018.

Norman, Philip. *Rave On: The Biography of Buddy Holly.* New York: Simon & Schuster, 1996.

Oglesby, Christopher. *Fire in the Water, Earth in the Air: Legends of West Texas Music.* Austin: University of Texas Press, 2006.

Overton, James. "Enhancing Inmate Life Through Prison Press." United Press interview with Benjamin Lach. *Ludington Daily News* (Ludington, MI), September 10, 1975.

Pelley, Scott. *Truth Worth Telling: A Reporter's Search for Meaning in the Stories of Our Times.* New York: Hanover Square Press, 2019.

Pettit, Burle. *A Boyhood Dream Realized: Half a Century of Texas Culture, One Newspaper Column at a Time.* Denton: University of North Texas Press, 2019.

Pickett, Al. *Mighty, Mighty Matadors: Estacado High School, Integration, and a Championship Season.* College Station: Texas A&M University Press, 2017.

Pickett, Carroll, with Carlton Stowers. *Within These Walls: Memoirs of a Death House Chaplain.* New York: St. Martin's Press, 2002.

Privett, Tony. *Failure Is Not an Option: Delbert McDougal: A Developer's Unconventional Wisdom.* San Antonio: Historical Publishing Network, 2007.

Renaud, Jorge Antonio. *Behind the Walls: A Guide for Families and Friends of Texas Prison Inmates.* Denton: University of North Texas Press, 2002.

Reynolds, Bill. *Lost Summer: The '67 Red Sox and the Impossible Dream.* New York: Warner Books, 1992.

Reynolds, Carl. "Texas Criminal Justice Chronology, 1984–2004." Remarks, ABA Justice Kennedy Commission, 2004.

Rich, John. "Lach, Winston Are New Officers of Psych. Society." *The Echo* (Huntsville, TX), June/July 1980.

Righi, Brian. *Supernatural Texas: A Field Guide.* Atglen, PA: Schiffer Publishing, 2009.

Rigler, Lewis C., and Judyth W. Rigler. *In the Line of Duty: Reflections of a Texas Ranger Private.* Denton: University of North Texas Press, 1995.

Rose, Francis L., and Russell W. Strandtmann. *Wildflowers of the Llano Estacado.* Dallas: Taylor Publishing Company, 1986.

Rosen, Fred. *There but for the Grace of God.* New York: Harper, 2007.

Roth, Mitchel P. *Convict Cowboys: The Untold History of the Texas Prison Rodeo.* Denton: University of North Texas Press, 2016.

Rushing, Jane Gilmore, and Kline A. Nall. *Evolution of a University: Texas Tech's First Fifty Years.* Austin: Madrona Press, 1975.

Rylander, Kent. *The Behavior of Texas Birds.* Austin: University of Texas Press, 2002.

———. *Blind Angela.* Flyleaf Medias, 2017.

———. *The Mustangs of Cotopaxi and other stories.* 2016.

Ryzuk, Mary. *The Gainesville Ripper: A True Story of Ultimate Horror.* New York: St. Martin's Paperbacks, 1995.

Sands, Stella. *Murder at Yale: The True Story of a Beautiful Grad Student and a Cold-Blooded Crime.* New York: St. Martin's Paperbacks, 2010.

Schreiber, Flora Rheta. *Sybil.* Chicago: Henry Regnery Company, 1973.

Scofield, Rebecca. *Outriders: Rodeo at the Fringes of the American West.* Seattle: University of Washington Press, 2019.

Sherman, Casey. *Search for the Boston Strangler.* New York: Time Warner, 2003.

Sherwood, Derek. *Who Killed Betsy? Uncovering Penn State University's Most Notorious Unsolved Crime.* Pine Grove Press, 2011.

Shropshire, Mike. *Runnin' with the Big Dogs: The True, Unvarnished Story of the Texas-Oklahoma Football Wars*. New York: William Morrow, 2006.

Silva, José. *A Texas Murder Case*. Laredo: Silva UltraMind Systems and Avlis Publishing.

Smallwood, Scott. "The Price of Murder." *Chronicle of Higher Education*, September 12, 2003.

Stevenson, Robert Louis. *Dr. Jekyll and Mr. Hyde*. New York: Pocket Books, 2005.

Stone, Robert B. *José Silva: The Man Who Tapped the Secrets of the Human Mind and the Method He Used*. Tiburon, CA: H.J. Kramer, Inc., 1990.

Stout, Martha. *The Sociopath Next Door*. New York: Broadway Books, 2005.

Sublett, Jesse. *1960s Austin Gangsters: Organized Crime That Rocked the Capital*. Charleston, SC: The History Press, 2015.

Swanson, William. *Dial M: The Murder of Carol Thompson*. St. Paul, MN: Borealis Books, The Minnesota Historical Society Press, 2006.

Swindle, Howard. "Alert Prof, NT Ex Nabs Tech Suspect." *The Campus Chat*. North Texas State University (Denton, TX), March 20, 1968.

Television Factbook. 1968–1969 ed. Washington, DC: Television Digest, Inc., 1968.

Thompson, Jim. *The Killer Inside Me*. London: Orion Publishing, 2002.

Tucker, Elizabeth. *Campus Legends: A Handbook*. Westport, CT: Greenwood Press, 2005.

TV Guide. Program listings, December 2–8, 1967.

Upton, Richard. "Editor Wins Levi's." *The Echo* (Huntsville, TX), December 1976.

Weinstein, Fannie, and Melinda Wilson. *The Coed Call Girl Murder*. New York: St. Martin's, 1997.

Wheeler, David. *The Lubbock Lights*. New York: Award Books, 1977.

Whitburn, Joel. *The Billboard Book of Top 40 Hits*. New York: Billboard Publications, 1985.

Willett, Jim, and Ron Rozelle. *Warden: Prison Life and Death from the Inside Out*. Albany, TX: Bright Sky Press, 2004.

Williams, Docia Schultz. *Phantoms of the Plains: Tales of West Texas Ghosts*. Plano, TX: Republic of Texas Press, 1996.

Williams, Scott. *Haunted Texas: A Travel Guide*. Guilford, CT: Globe Pequot Press, 2007.

Williams, Shelton L. *Summer of '66*. Denton, TX: Zone Press, 2007.

Wolfe, Linda. *The Professor and the Prostitute*. New York: Ballantine Books, 1986.

THE ECHO (HUNTSVILLE, TX) EDITORIALS WRITTEN BY BENJAMIN LACH

"Peace in Mind," 1975.

"Music Is Pleasant to the Ear," January 1977.

"Growing of Age," February 1977.

"Roots," February 1977.

"There Is a Chance for Ex-Offenders," April 1977.

"To Vote or Not to Vote?" April 1979.

"Scared Straight Approach," August/September 1979.

"Head-Running," May 1981.

"Men and Rehabilitation," April 1981.

"Danny's Home" (short story), May 1981.

"Are We All in This Together?" July 1981

"Making It on Furlough," date unknown.

"Sports Festival Draws Attention," February 1982.

"Having Cake, Eating It Too" (with Charles Gregory), September 1982.

"Videos Facilitate Communications," March/April 1983.

"About Prisoners: Myth or Fact?" May/June 1983.

"Prison Rodeo in Perspective," September 1983.

"On Going Straight," September 1983.

LEGAL DOCUMENTS

Examining Trial Transcript, No. 464, *The State of Texas v. Benjamin Lach*, Justice of the Peace Court, Precinct 6, Lubbock County, Texas, March 25, 1968.

Indictment, No. 11308, *The State of Texas v. Benjamin Lach*, Murder with Malice, April 16, 1968.

Question and Answer Transcript, Preliminary Sanity Hearing, No. 11,308, *The State of Texas v. Benjamin Lach*, 99th District Court, Lubbock County, Texas, July Term, 1968.

Decree of Present Insanity Commitment to Rusk State Hospital and Declaration of Mistrial on All Other Issues, No. 11,308, *The State of Texas v. Benjamin Lach*, 99th District Court, Lubbock County, Texas, December 31, 1968.

Order Changing Venue, No. 11,308, *The State of Texas v. Benjamin Lach*, 99th District Court, Lubbock County, Texas, May 28, 1970.

Motion to Suppress, and Prohibit Use Thereof by the State, of the Alleged Confession of Defendant, *The State of Texas v. Benjamin Lach*, Criminal District Court No. 1, Tarrant County, Texas.

Motion to Suppress and Prohibit the Asking for, Assessment of, or Making Reference to a Death Penalty, *The State of Texas v. Benjamin Lach*, Criminal District Court No. 1, Tarrant County, Texas.

Sentence Hearing Proceedings, No. 80660, *The State of Texas v. Benjamin Lach*, December 9, 1970.

Verdict and Judgment, Sentence, No. 80660, *The State of Texas v. Benjamin Lach*, December 15, 1970.

MUSIC AND FILM

Lubbock Lights. Directed and produced by Amy Maner and George Sledge. Lubbock: 289 Films, 2005.

Mac Davis. "Texas in My Rear View Mirror." *Stop and Smell the Roses*, 1974.

OTHER SOURCES

"1967 Suffolk University commencement program (all schools)." Suffolk University Commencements, 1967.

Abilene Reporter-News

The Activist Forum 1, no. 3 (May 1968)

Amarillo Globe Times

Ancestry.com

Austin American-Statesman

Big Spring Herald

The Boston Globe

Bulletin of Texas Technological College. Forty-second annual general catalog with announcements for 1967–1968. Part I, General Information and Degree Programs. Vol. 43, no. 2 (February 1967).

Bulletin of Texas Technological College. Forty-second annual general catalog with announcements for 1967–1968. Part II, Courses and Curricula. Vol. 43, no. 4 (April 1967).

Bulletin of Texas Tech University. Undergraduate catalog with announcements for 1976–1977. Vol. 52, no. 6 (June 1976).

Campus Chat (North Texas State University)

Corpus Christi Caller-Times

The Daily Texan (University of Texas at Austin)

The Daily Toreador (Texas Tech University)

The Dallas Morning News

Denton Record-Chronicle

The Echo (Huntsville, TX)

findagrave.com

Fort Worth Star-Telegram

The Galveston Daily News

Georgetown Advocate

Handbook of Texas Online

Intelius.com

José Silva website. jose-silva.net

La Ventana. Yearbook. Lubbock: Texas Tech University, 1968.

Lubbock Avalanche-Journal

Lubbock County Court records

Lubbock Online.com

Lubbock Police Department Offense Report #11734

Lubbock Police Department Supplementary Reports, December 5, 1967–March 27, 1968

The Mexia News

The Pampa Daily News

PeopleFinders.com

Recordsregistry.com

Rusk State Hospital Handbook

Sentrylink.com

The Sherman Democrat

Texas Almanac 1966–1967. Dallas: A. H. Belo Corporation, 1966. The Portal to Texas History. University of North Texas Libraries. https://texashistory.unt.edu/ark:/67531/metapth113808/.

Texas Almanac 1968–1969. Dallas: A. H. Belo Corporation, 1968. The Portal to Texas History. University of North Texas Libraries. https://texashistory.unt.edu/ark:/67531/metapth113809/.

Texas Almanac 1970–1971. Dallas: A. H. Belo Corporation, 1970. The Portal to Texas History. University of North Texas Libraries. https://texashistory.unt.edu/ark:/67531/metapth113810/:

Texas College Guide. 2006 edition. Austin: Texas Monthly Publishing, 2006.

Texas Prison Museum, https://www.txprisonmuseum.org/

Texas State Historical Association, tshaonline.org

Texas Tech Southwest Collection/Special Collections Library. Photographs. Lubbock, Texas,

Texas Tech undergraduate catalog, 2002–2003. Lubbock: Texas Tech University, 2002.

Texas Tech University, www.ttu.edu

Texas Tech University Police Department, https://www.depts.

ttu.edu/ttpd/

Texas Tech v. Rice. football game program, November 4, 1967.

Texas Techsan alumni magazine

ufocasebook.com.

The University Daily (Lubbock, TX). Texas Tech University student newspaper.

Virtualubbock.com

Weather Underground, wunderground.com

Wikipedia.com

Yahoo People Search

AUTHOR INTERVIEWS

Judge J. Blair Cherry, in person interview by Alan Burton, June 3, 2003, and June 13, 2005; email correspondence with Alan Burton, June 24, 2003, December 20, 2004, June 8, 2005, July 17, 2005, January 25, 2007, January 26, 2007, March 22, 2007, August 21, 2007, and September 18, 2007.

Dr. Kenneth Davis, email correspondence with Alan Burton, November 21, 2004.

Dr. Bill Dean, email correspondence with Alan Burton, April 5, 2005.

Alton Griffin, in person interview with Alan Burton, June 25, 2003.

Larry Hagood, in person interview with Alan Burton, June 14, 2005.

Walt Hagood, in person interview with Alan Burton, June 16, 2005.

F. E. "Butch" Hargrave, telephone interview with Alan Burton, 2007.

Roy McQueen, email correspondence with Alan Burton, November 29, 2004.

Freda McVay, email correspondence with Alan Burton, date unavailable.

Tom Purdom, email correspondence with Alan Burton, February 1, 2007, and April 9, 2011.

Dr. Kent Rylander, email correspondence with Alan Burton, November 17, 2004, and November 20, 2004.

President David Schmidly, email correspondence, telephone interview with Alan Burton, January 24, 2006.

Jackie Smith, telephone interview with Alan Burton, date unavailable.
Frank Wiley, telephone interview with Alan Burton, date unavailable.
Jim Willett, email correspondence with Alan Burton, 2008.

ORAL HISTORIES

Alton Griffin. Interview by Fred Allison. Tape recording. Lubbock,
  Texas. July 2, 1998, and July 10, 1998. Oral History Collection.
  Southwest Collection/Special Collections Library, Texas Tech
  University.
Dr. Kent Rylander. Interview by David Marshall. Tape recording.
  Junction, Texas. March 22, 2004. Oral History Collection. Southwest
  Collection/Special Collections Library, Texas Tech University.

ABOUT THE AUTHORS

Alan Burton's professional writing career spans nearly forty years. His work has been honored by the Associated Press, Texas School Public Relations Association, and Oklahoma College Public Relations Association.

His resume includes forty years of experience in the media/communications field; he recently retired as special assistant to the president and director of University Communications at Southeastern Oklahoma State University. He was associated with the university in Durant, Oklahoma, for twenty-three years in various capacities. Before that, he was director of Community Relations for eleven years for the Sherman (Texas) Independent School District. He began his career as sports editor at the *Sherman Democrat*. Burton is a Sherman native.

Burton is a 1979 graduate of Texas Tech University, where he earned a bachelor of arts degree in English.

This is his ninth book. His other books include *Til the Fat Lady Sings . . . Classic Texas Sports Quotes* (Texas Tech University Press, 1994); *Rave On . . . Classic Texas Music Quotes* (Texas Tech University Press, 1996); *Texas High School Hotshots . . . The Stars Before They Were Stars* (Republic of Texas Press, 2002); *Dallas Cowboys Quips and Quotes* (State House Press, 2006); *Pirates, Soldiers & Fat Little Girlfriends . . . More Classic Texas Sports Quotes* (Zone Press, 2010); *Squib-Kick It to a Fat Guy . . . and 699 more memorable quotes from the Playbook of Coach Mike Leach* (Anarene Books, 2016); *Go to the Games with Humble – Kern Tips and the Golden Age of SWC Radio* (Anarene Books, 2019); and *Vol. II, Squib-Kick It to a Fat Guy . . . and 701 more memorable quotes from the Playbook of Coach Mike Leach* (Anarene Books, 2021).

Chuck Lanehart is a shareholder in the Lubbock firm of Chappell, Lanehart & Stangl, P.C., where he has practiced law since 1977. He is a 1977 graduate of Texas Tech University School of Law. He is board certified in the field of Criminal Law by the Texas Board of Legal Specialization.

Lanehart served as director of the State Bar of Texas, District 16, and as president of the Lubbock Area Bar Association (LABA). He was the founding editor of LABA's monthly publication, *The Lubbock Law Notes*. He was a founding member of the South Plains Trial Lawyers Association, and he is a life Fellow of the Texas Bar Foundation.

Lanehart is a former director of the Texas Criminal Defense Lawyers Association (TCDLA). TCDLA awarded him the President's Commendation for "Outstanding Service to the Citizen Accused" and also honored him with the President's Award for his service to the TCDLA's Strike Force. He is a charter member and former president of the Lubbock Criminal Defense Lawyers Association.

He has published numerous articles on legal history and legal ethics in various law journals. Since 2017, he has contributed regularly to the *Lubbock Avalanche-Journal* Sunday history series "Caprock Chronicles." The History Press has published three of Chuck's books: *Tragedy and Triumph on the Texas Plains* (2021), *Marvels of the Texas Plains* (2022), and *Evolution of the Texas Plains* (2023). Westerner's International awarded him the 2020 Coke Wood Award for the best published Western American history article, "Custer, Captive Girls and the Cheyenne on Sweetwater Creek."

In 2008, Lanehart was named among the "200 Most Influential People in the History of Lubbock" by the *Lubbock Avalanche-Journal*. In 2018, the Lubbock Area Bar Association presented him the Distinguished Lawyer Award, the Bar's highest honor.

Printed in the USA
CPSIA information can be obtained
at www.ICGtesting.com
LVHW050943240124
769414LV00002BB/283